D0555925

HAUNTED
INDEPENDENCE,
OREGON

HAUNTED
INDEPENDENCE, OREGON

MARILYN MORTON

Haunted
America

Published by Haunted America
A Division of The History Press
Charleston, SC 29403
www.historypress.net

Copyright © 2013 by Marilyn Morton
All rights reserved

First published 2013

Manufactured in the United States

ISBN 978.1.60949.872.6

Library of Congress CIP data applied for.

Notice: The information in this book is true and complete to the best of our knowledge. It is offered without guarantee on the part of the author or The History Press. The author and The History Press disclaim all liability in connection with the use of this book.

All rights reserved. No part of this book may be reproduced or transmitted in any form whatsoever without prior written permission from the publisher except in the case of brief quotations embodied in critical articles and reviews.

CONTENTS

CONTENTS

FOREWORD

Human history is about stories and tales of adventure, people and events told person to person over generations. In Independence, our history is wrapped up in the stories told—neighbor to friend, resident to visitor, parent to child, handed down from one generation to another.

Our community has a rich and interesting heritage, including native peoples, early pioneers, riverboats, hop festivals, an agricultural center, wars, brothels, depressions and daily living mixed with the personalities and events that over years become history, with all its twists and turns.

While I have never personally seen a ghost, people I know and trust have seen and heard things that cannot be explained. I'm not willing to say that they don't exist.

I like to think that our stories of ghosts and our connections to other dimensions allow bits of Independence history and the individual events of lives gone before us to come "alive" with each and every story, stories that provide a portal in time, a window into the lives of the people who were players in years gone past.

Enjoy the stories, revel in the tales of bygone years and then visit, walk and experience Independence with a new pair of eyes and with knowledge of the stories. Who knows what—or should I say whom—you'll meet…

—John McArdle
Mayor of Independence

CHAPTER 1
COMMUNITY STORIES

The haunting of Independence surely started before wagon trains and white men arrived. We could say with confidence that there were stories Native Americans swapped around campfires and during the drudgery of long treks. But sadly, none of those were forwarded to the settlers, and if they survive, it is only through tribal tradition. The earliest stories remain with the original holders and tellers.

Were stories passed to individuals from the early pioneer influx? Undoubtedly. I certainly have been given some closely guarded family lore to hold. But, as is the credo of many family groups, stories were never told outside that circle. After all, "It's nobody else's business!"

So, before the formal story of Independence begins, I'm going to break the silence on one of my stories.

I believe that stories are the foundation of community. Survival in the earliest days depended on the sanctity of the family unit, and it was within those bounds that stories resided. As we progressed to a broader platform of tribal groups, the stories of individuals and families became the lore of the tribe.

Tribes became villages and then small towns, evolving eventually into cities of unimaginable size. Though stories linger in neighborhoods, a mega-city generates its own stories, often on nightly news. The charm of the early tales is lost in the news and twitter flashes of today.

But to declare all stories forgotten, unimportant or commercialized is to overlook one fertile field left where stories are still the energy of community. That is in the small town.

My town, Independence, Oregon, is such a town. I first moved to Independence almost twenty-three years ago (by many standards, I'm still a newbie), and I became engaged in a lot of volunteer work. That meant I met neighbors and community members who took time out of their days to read to kids, volunteer in classrooms, take preschoolers on field trips, work on festivals and serve on committees. We talked, and the stories began to flow.

I learned about the family who lived in an old farmhouse they couldn't afford to heat above fifty-five degrees. The kids who slept upstairs had an icy rime on their covers when their breaths would condense and cause a small snow flurry during the coldest hours.

I heard about the unpredictable tragedy of a young boy killed while riding his bike on a sidewalk far back from the road. A car jumped the road, plowed through a backyard and ended up across a neighborhood sidewalk at the wrong moment—boy on bike and out of control car met.

One story I've shared myself is that of the woman who developed recipes for cooking nutria. They are an imported invasive scourge. Such was the population in her yard that she worked up her own recipes for baked and fried nutria. No, it doesn't taste like chicken (and I report this NOT through personal experience), but it is awfully greasy. The way the woman told it to me, and how I repeat it, is that nutria meat is "greazy."

Stories originate at every level, from international politics to unique family fables. Stories shape nations and individuals. Stories, say the experts, are founded on a grain of truth. National stories may honor heroes and dogged perseverance. Family stories shape new generations with tales of the honor, strength or uniqueness of ancestors. The stories from Independence have a flavor of the otherworldly or the unexplainable. Independence has many stories to tell, and readers will find them liberally sprinkled through this book. I believe in stories, in their power and in their ability to build community.

CHAPTER 2
ONE OF MY OWN STORIES

My great-great-grandmother was born in the 1830s and had, by family account, flaming red hair, thick and curly. She and my great-great-grandfather lived in a sod house in the plains. A local native tribe was settled in the same area. It didn't take long before the red hair became the talk of the tribe's young men. I was cautioned that her scalp was never in danger of removal but that locks of her long red hair were wanted for souvenirs and decoration. It became a regular occurrence that young native men appeared at the unglazed window of the sod home. At first, perhaps, it was just to look for some stray hairs. Then the lookers became more bold and came to the front door, where they would be standing when she went out to do chores. My great-great grandmother was understandably frightened. This went on for several days, and finally, not willing to be made prisoner in her own home any longer, she hoisted a large cast-iron pan. Pushing back the door flap, there again was a young man. And completely without fear, my relative conked him in the head with the skillet. He was not terribly injured but quite stunned. According to the tale, from then on, the native population gave her a wide berth.

How and why did this story appeal to me? First, I was proud of my ancestress for her bravery. The story also implied that she was a good-looking woman, telling me that I come from a blood line that produces beautiful women. This certainly gave hope to my then gangly prepubescent self. It also tells me that she was courageous. Not only would she defend herself but would also do so when her husband was obviously not around and not part

The only remaining sod school house in Decatur County, Kansas. Jos Young, circa 1907. *Courtesy Library of Congress.*

of the story. He was mentioned only as being a resident of the sod house. A sod house—how cool! That branded my family as real pioneers, and pretty inventive ones, too. The native tribe that lived close by? Another sign of an intrepid family. They dared to live right on the edge of "civilization." I was disappointed that the story didn't include children. I do remember deciding that she was probably pretty young and barely married. Another point for chaste family stock. That story made me feel good about where I came from and gave me hope for a solid future.

As an adult I look back and think, red hair, curly locks, sure…that's what the young men were after. But it just shows that stories can be tailored for age-appropriate use. I didn't need to be frightened by ugly possibilities, and at the time I believed the story without dispute. As my maturity revealed a possible deeper texture to the story, I simply observed the possibility and retold the story to my children, just as I had heard it. The reward? My daughter said, "We had cool ancestors!"

CHAPTER 3

LEARNING THE STORIES

Volunteer work often took me to our downtown. We have a three-block main street lined with beautiful older buildings. I am told that every form of architecture—except French Provincial—is represented there. It became a joke that I was a frequent "street walker," always going from business to business delivering posters, flyers and information about local events. There is such pleasure for me in visiting my friends in their businesses, so delivery of a poster was never a static event. We would chat about business, local politics and things happening downtown.

It did not take long before the stories relative to those buildings were being shared. Early on, I heard about the spirit in the basement of one place, the boy who bounced a ball over and over, and the voices heard in the steepled area of a particular edifice.

In those days, I viewed myself as an old-style telephone operator who sat at a switchboard and plugged in wires to connect callers. I carried the stories and the news around and would mention new information as I went on my route. This drew out more data, and it often went something like this:

I would begin, "Hi! I was just next door and heard that they think they have somebody getting into their basement. They keep hearing noises. Are you aware of anything here?"

To which they would reply, "You know, that guy next door is new. He's only been here for a couple of years. I'm surprised he didn't start hearing noises before now! Every owner of the building has heard those same noises.

They go looking and never find anything. I've always heard that the original owner never really left. He's mad about something."

More walking, more talking, more stories. The theme of haunting began to emerge. The more I heard, the more I asked. At one time, I was told a community college student had written a term paper on the ghost stories of Independence. I secured a copy—which has since gone mysteriously missing—and read it through. Many of the stories I had been hearing were there, intact just as I had heard them. A few others were older tales, which I have since also heard from townspeople. There was nothing completely new to me, which itself is telling of the power of stories.

Later on, when the Ghost Walk began, I had a decision to make about validation and documentation. Stories that exist in small towns always have a kernel of truth, often more. But they also gather, in the retelling, the texture of personal opinion, the depth of family honor upheld or threatened and verbal modernization where it helps the listener understand. Finally, my criteria for a story to be told on the Ghost Walk had to be: "I heard that…" I sought *living* stories to share with people. Rarely do I reference the college term paper, because those are mere words on page. Frequently I am gratified by someone on a Ghost Walk saying, "Yup, that's pretty much the way my grandmother told it to me."

CHAPTER 4

THE FOUNDATION IS LAID

In the late 1990s, the economy was strong, and a downtown renaissance began in earnest. Some of the oldest buildings were renovated, which did two things. The restoration work revealed original architectural aspects that were often uniform and always lovely. And, the stories—perhaps even the ghosts themselves—were stirred into vibrant life.

Before we cover any more spectral ground, let me take you back to early pioneer Independence.

Independence was established in 1845—that's fourteen years before Oregon became a state. But people had been arriving by wagon train before that. Independence lays claim to being the "end of the Oregon Trail." However, in fairness, we share that distinction with several other places, chief among them Oregon City, Oregon. After a minor e-mail altercation with a city commissioner from Oregon City, we have decided sharing is just fine!

The city was originally organized on a donation land claim held by Elvin Thorp, who named the town Independence after his hometown of Independence, Missouri. He came via covered wagon from established Independence (east) to brand-new Independence (west). The claim for Independence that Thorp made was north of Ash Creek—now the north entrance to Independence. Ash Creek and the Willamette River make a "T" shape where they join. Thorp's town of Independence was just north of the "T," bounded on two sides by bodies of water.

Wagon trains began rolling west in the early 1850s. A popular destination was Independence. It didn't take long before Independence was being organized as a city. Records show that two different "towns" of Independence were developed separately. In one location, Elvin A. Thorp was bringing together a community. And not far away, Henry Hill was gathering his own group of residents. Describing this process in more detail is an excerpt from the Preserve America website—Independence is a Preserve America city (http://www.preserveamerica.gov/PAcommunity-independenceOR.html):

Independence, Oregon, (population 9,375) was founded (twice) in the Willamette River Valley by settlers who had traveled the Oregon Trail, departing from Independence, Missouri. Elvin A. Thorp founded a town when he arrived in 1845 on the west bank of the Willamette River, just north of Ash Creek. Two years later Henry Hill arrived. He staked a claim (and opened a store) just south of Ash Creek through the Donation Land Claim Act (a forerunner of the Homestead Act), and then left for the gold fields of California. Upon his return in 1867, he found that "Thorp's Town of Independence" had been mostly destroyed by a flood in 1861. He plotted out a town on the higher ground south of Ash Creek, which came to be known as "Henry Hill's Town of Independence," and the two towns were merged when they incorporated in 1885. The area that was once "Thorp's Town of Independence" is now known as "Old Town."

Independence began in 1845, when Elvin Thorp first put down official roots. Finally, in 1885, the town was incorporated.
Amenities arrived on the following schedule:

- train, 1885
- electricity, 1890
- city water, 1891
- telephone and telegraph, 1892

In an April 8, 1917 *Sunday Oregonian* newspaper article, the "absorption" of Thorp's Town of Independence is noted:

TOWN EXTENDS ITS LIMITS
Independence Takes in Northern Suburb and Growth is Likely
INDEPENDENCE, OR, April 7 (Special)
The business portion of Independence has extended its limits within the past month to North Independence, formerly known as Thorps Town of Independence. For 30 years that part of the city has been without a

business house of any kind, while in former years the only store located in Independence was in this northern part of town.

Other business locations are being sought by local men, and the business section will no doubt extend several blocks to the north.

Several thousands of dollars have been expended by the county during the past year in constructing a concrete bridge and fill in that part of the city, and about two miles of paved road was also constructed.

There are no known stories about any ghosts or hauntings from the time the towns were forming. However, echoes of difficult days are preserved in sounds and voices heard in some of the downtown locations. Flood and fire were the mostly commonly endured natural disasters. Period newspaper accounts also talk of farm accidents, hunting accidents, drownings, runaway teams and more. It was obviously a hard life.

From early times, Independence and its residents have been intrepid. It did not take long before a promising cash crop was discovered in hops. Native Americans had been growing and using hops for many years, and the pioneers caught on. Hops were cultivated with vigor and determination. During the first fifty years of the twentieth century, Independence was known as the "Historical Hop Capital of the World." Post–World War II, hop production waned. We'll talk about that on the Ghost Walk when we visit the mini-hop yard behind the library.

Hops are thriving in Independence, and in 2011, the city once again playfully declared itself the "Hop Capital of the World." No, there is not universal acknowledgement of that title, but just wait. There will be. As Mayor John McArdle says, we are "can-do folks," and we "move at the speed of Independence."

HOPS AND HISTORY

During the prime hop years (pre-1950), Independence hosted an annual Hop Fiesta, or Hop Festival, celebrating the end of the harvest. Growing and harvesting hops took a whole season and lots of workers, as evidenced by the following newspaper article:

Morning Oregonian, Portland, OR, September 6, 1905
Polk County Full of Pickers

Annual Hop Harvest Carnival has Begun

Independence, OR, Sept. 5.—(Special.)—Independence and the surrounding country are alive with hoppickers and picking began in a number of yards today. Picking will commence in others tomorrow, and still others on Thursday and by Friday will be general. For a while there was some fear of a shortage of pickers for the reason they have not arrived as early as last year. All of a sudden, however, the sunbonnet and Mother Hubbard and Roosevelt families have put in an appearance and every train is bringing more, while the dust-enveloped roads leading toward Independence are strewn with teams drawing families and leading the family cow.

Evidences of the annual hop harvest carnival are to be seen on every hand. Stores run wide open till late at night and clerks are taxed to their limit in waiting on pickers getting ready for camp-life and song and music resound from several resorts.

More attention than usual has been paid to the amusement feature for pickers this year and every yard of any size is provided with an amusement or dance hall. The E. Clemens Horst yard of 450 acres has never promoted amusements until this year. A new hall, 100 x 50 feet, has been dedicated to pickers on the ground without awaiting for picking to commence.

The amusement event that promises to eclipse all others is the opening of the new hall at the Kreb Bros. yards, known as "The Trail," Saturday night of this week. The Krebs have provided a hall with a capacity for 800 couples and preparations are on to entertain 10,000 people at the dedication Saturday night. The opening of the picking season and dedication of the Krebs amusement hall promises to be historic in hop circles. Arrangements have been made for a special train of 13 cars out of Portland on Thursday. The Krebs opening Saturday night is the talk among the pickers of other yards who will turn out and many are expected from different towns throughout the valley.

The Siletz Indians to the number of 100 have arrived and being denied whisky by the town authorities are creating very little commotion. The present outlook does not indicate an over-supply of pickers, though no fears are entertained of a shortage provided rain does not set in.

At the present stage the prospect for a big yield is not promising, though the bur of the hop was never in better condition at harvest time.

Camps were set up at each of the largest hop yards to accommodate workers who moved with the crops. Many folks in Independence come from families who were our early agricultural workers. They recall being

Picking Hops in the Willamette Valley. *Courtesy OSU Special Collections.*

"home schooled" in the hop rows. They also recall the whole family working, with women and girls in long dresses. I have spoken with many people whose early years were spent in the hop harvest. They hail from all local cultures. Our museum and library conduct a constantly evolving project as they gather stories and artifacts from that era still well remembered. Harvesting hops was not only a family endeavor but also a way for young people to learn the discipline and rigors of work. Hop farmers sent their own children out into the fields to experience what the hired workers did. Names of important families are preserved in the community landscape: Cooper, Sperling, Hill, Butler and more. These are celebrated pioneer names that still have living representatives proud of their heritage.

At the end of the season, with hops harvested and sold, it was time to celebrate. The Hop Festival of the early twentieth-century was a huge event, bringing thousands of people into the downtown area. Historical photos and reports tell us that the original Hop Festival, impromptu from the beginning and formally organized beginning in the early 1930s, was a widely attended event. Thousands of people thronged the streets. A parade seven blocks long opened the activities. Townsfolk, cars, soldiers, politicians, cows, horses, dogs and, of course, the Hop Queen and her

Court—everybody paraded. The parade ended in the Hop Bowl. The jubilation went on for hours. There was barely room to move downtown for the throngs of people. Everyone partied, celebrating the end of the harvest and all the hard work that came with it.

More stories about those early years will be told in the narrative as we take the Ghost Walk. For now, let's fast-forward to the year 2001. Remember the downtown renaissance? The mayor wanted to find a way to celebrate that effort, and he had an idea.

CHAPTER 5
STORIES ARE CREATED ALL THE TIME

THE STORY OF THE HOP FESTIVAL, INDEPENDENCE STYLE

Here is a first taste of a community story, all about the beginning of the Independence Hop and Heritage Festival. In 2001, John McArdle brought together a group of folks enthusiastic about Independence. They shared a common interest in seeing it thrive, both economically and culturally. The city would soon finish the first phase of its downtown renaissance. Mayor McArdle wanted a public opening of the re-done downtown, and it seemed fitting to have an event to mark the coming occasion.

In May, the group met, and the challenge was laid out by the mayor:

Back in the day, there used to be a Hop Festival or Hop Fiesta in this town. It was a grand end-of-harvest party to which an entire town was invited. Let's do it again.

Could we make it happen? First thing to do was stake out a date. The group opted for September 29, 2001, the last Saturday of the month. Plans were made and action followed with a summer-long flurry.

September arrived, and everything was coming together. A meeting was planned for September 12. But the group that arrived that evening was somber and afraid. What to do? Have a party in the midst of the overwhelming national sorrow caused by the horror of September 11?

Mayor McArdle came to that meeting too. He let the murmuring go for a little, then dropped in a few words: "Don't let the sons of bitches win. Don't let them change your plans. Just get on with everything."

Hop Festival's coming. *Courtesy BestinOregon.com.*

And so we did. At 10:00 a.m. on festival day, out onto the karaoke stage, unplanned, came a solitary woman. She flipped on her amps and lifted the mike to begin an *a capella* version of the national anthem. People came out of stores into the streets, seeking a waving flag. As they found one, they turned to the flag, put hands on hearts and silently saluted as the woman's song concluded.

Then the festival began. Families came. Music filled the street, the food smelled great, the sun was warm and people felt safe and happy. They danced, laughed, sang and enjoyed the community. In that first year, the local farmers' market stayed open all day. Food was cooked on the street and served in traditional ways. A local favorite was corn on the cob slathered in mayonnaise and then sprinkled with paprika and hot pepper. Square-dancers performed. Musicians on stage filled the downtown with song. The only thing lacking the first year was a beer garden, but that omission was soon corrected. In fact, that aspect of the festival has evolved into a beer garden, a home brew competition and, coming soon, a wet hops beer fest. "Wet hops" beer is brew that is flavored with fresh, green, undried hops. It is a unique, from-the-field flavor that is becoming very popular.

The festival has continued and flourished since then. Many features have been added to the event, including the Ghost Walk on festival eve.

PART 2, SAME STORY, THE GHOST WALK

The Ghost Walk was added to the fun of Hop Festival in its second year, 2002. The first inkling of the Ghost Walk, though, occurred when I was out of state. Here's *that* story:

It was April 2002. My daughter was devastated. She was going on a band trip to San Francisco, but in a domino-like chain of events, including a date change for the senior prom, the trip was cancelled.

I was at the meeting when the Band Boosters had to give the bad news to students. It was a somber group that left the band room that evening. When we got home, I stopped my daughter and said, "Here's my credit card. Book us a trip to San Francisco." It didn't take long before she agreed that it would be fun and started to check the Internet for transportation and lodging.

Two weeks later, we left for San Francisco. She had booked us in a motel at Fisherman's Wharf. One evening, while we strolled along the wharf, we spotted a sign that said, "Take the Barbary Coast Ghost Walk." In one of those unique moments of shared inspiration, we looked at each other and said, "We could do that in Independence."

The trip was great, and we were back home in time for a Hop Festival meeting. I brought up the idea of a Ghost Walk, and it met a very positive response. But something not unexpected also happened: "You have to do all the work." Everyone was already busy on event planning, so I agreed to chair the now fledgling Ghost Walk.

That first year, I visited three businesses that I felt had the most dramatic stories. These three were chosen because they also had what I felt were the most well-known stories. The first reaction of the owners of those businesses was probably confusion. What do you mean? What's a Ghost Walk? Why would people want to hear stories like that? I promised to do the advance work, if they would be on hand for a short session of storytelling. Just ten minutes, just a couple stories. Please?

That first year, there were just three stops on the Ghost Walk. It was a mere 10 percent of what it is now. The appeal of being exclusive was helpful, as was the promise of having just the single task of storytelling. The original three were Town & Country Hardware, Ash Creek Animal Clinic and Lyon Lodge #29, the local Masonic lodge. The plan was that at 7:00 p.m., I would begin telling stories in the lodge, which was upstairs over the hardware store. Stories would be shared in the lodge room. Then the Ghost Walkers—if we had any at all—would be escorted downstairs to the hardware store to hear the proprietor tell his tales. Finally, our little troop would head for the animal clinic, one block away, and hear the last story. And that would be that.

An article had run in the newspaper about a new event in Independence, something called a "Ghost Walk." Beyond that article, we relied on word of mouth and a few posters to do our advertising job.

The evening of the first Ghost Walk, September 27, 2002, I went to a downtown restaurant to have dinner with a friend. I remember telling her, "I'm hoping there will be at least thirty people down here for the Ghost Walk. That would feel like a success for the first year."

I had confirmed that my storytellers were in place and buildings were open and ready to receive guests. Downtown felt active that night, and it was a balmy early fall evening. After saying goodbye to my friend, I started walking toward the Masonic lodge. It didn't take long to realize there was a knot of people outside of the lodge, perhaps seventy-five or eighty. More success than I'd imagined!

Arriving at the lodge, I found that I had miscounted. There were closer to two hundred people downstairs, and the lodge hall, which holds over one hundred, was already full. People had come up to a half hour early to be in time for that first Ghost Walk.

I had a quick strategy meeting with a couple of the lodge members who agreed to manage folks. They would send me our guests in groups the size to fill the lodge hall and ask others to wait. I would speak about fifteen minutes, including a question-and-answer session, and then send them on to the next stop. A runner was sent to the other two sites to let them know about the crowd and to let them know guests would come in two or three waves.

THE FIRST TELLING OF THE MASONIC LODGE STORY

The first story told at the Masonic lodge was mostly extemporaneous. Everyone thought the first year would be pretty easygoing.

The Masonic lodge was built in 1892 by Lemuel Lyon, who went on to become a big deal in Dallas, Oregon. It is the first building to have been constructed on this site. Years ago, it stood next to Independence Creamery, our first big local industry. But the creamery burned down in a spectacular fire near the turn of the century. Fire has been discussed before. The creamery was another casualty of fire that just happens. Arson? Probably not. Just natural causes. As for the Masonic Lodge, because the lodge is brick on all sides, even the one that adjoined the creamery, it was spared from the fire.

Many groups have met in this building, including Job's Daughters, a group for young women; the Blue Lodge of Masons for men; and an Eastern Star group for women. There has been a DeMolay group here, and when you tour the building, you will see their equipment still stored here, including capes and swords.

Some of the Masons have seen and heard interesting things here. Stories from years past are scarce, but that may be a result of the way Masonry is organized, not secretive but certainly loyal. Lights go on and off, there are footsteps heard in the attic where nobody has gone for years and bats often find their way into this space, but their point of entry has never been located.

Much of what the lodge has to tell is a historic tale. However, one of my friends, a Mason, says that he has seen ghostly figures escorting various group members around as they do their ritual work in meetings. He has also looked down a dark stairwell and seen glowing eyes.

The unusual things that happen in downtown Independence are not threatening. The spookiness is impressive, but I believe the spirits mean no harm. At worst, it might be some activity that's a little mischievous. We don't seem to have evil, nasty or even naughty spirits. They must like our town as much as we do.

During the time I was speaking, the local news photographer was snapping pictures. As I exited the room to await entry of group number two, he called me over. "You've got to see this," he said with excitement. He showed me the pictures he'd taken with his digital camera. In the pictures, there is a light hovering near my head. As he snapped photo to photo, it became clear that the light was "circling" my head. I asked him if he would send me a copy of his photos. He agreed.

When I went in to speak to group two of the three I would have that night, the latest story—the glowing orbiting light—was added to the story. There was a conspiratorial pride in this group that the first folks hadn't been "let in" on this new element.

This was the first episode where an orb was photographed in the Masonic lodge. Since that night, hundreds of orbs have shown up in photos. There is no pattern to their appearance: sometimes the first person gets the best picture, sometimes the last. But it is evident that from year to year, the orb population has grown. Are we attracting visitors? Are "they" having their own Ghost Walk, and are we the ones being watched?

After hearing the lodge stories, the first group went into the basement of the hardware store to hear those tales, which will be detailed later. It is important to note that this is another building from which stories continue to surface.

Finally, the groups made it to the animal clinic and heard their story. Later, one of the veterinarians reported that they had done an official head count. There were 311 people on the first Ghost Walk, far more than I dared to expect.

PHOTOGRAPHS TAKEN BY THE NEWSMAN

I waited for those pictures taken in the lodge building to come from my photographer friend. They never did, so finally I visited the newspaper office. He came out with a sad look on his face to report that he had lost the photos. The paper had provided him with a new computer, he said, and he didn't realize that pushing "delete" meant erasure forever. Another piece of evidence lost!

Years later, when I was at the newspaper office again, I mentioned the unfortunate deletion of photographs. One of the staff came out and said, "I have to set the record straight. He didn't accidentally erase those pictures—he did it on purpose. He kept looking at them, knowing they were pretty strange. Finally he said, 'I don't want to be one of *those* reporters.' And he hit delete." In the interest of the higher side of his craft, the photographer had chosen to lose the pictures.

CHAPTER 6

THE GHOST WALK CREATES ITS OWN STORIES

The oddest thing that has ever happened to slim down the size of my group is their utter and complete disappearance. My big group was to begin their tour at the Masonic lodge. I herded them—about ninety folks—toward our destination. We stopped frequently to do hearing checks and to see that everyone was clustered together. At the bottom of the steps leading up to the lodge, I sent the bulk of that year's oversized group up into the lodge. About eighty people started up the stairs into the lodge that has more than enough capacity for them all.

Meanwhile, downstairs, the other ten or so folks left had decided not to manage the stairs. To our great surprise, one of the area's old-timers was seated outside talking with friends. He has a distinctive and rich voice that carries well. I heard him talking about one of the resident ghosts from two blocks away and made a spontaneous decision (the best kind on Ghost Walk night!). I asked him if he would mind starting his story over again for my now-small group of folks. He was happy to and told the story of Lerona, which is detailed later. Not only did he know the story, but he claimed to have seen Lerona in her usual environs—more than once.

These captivating treats make the Ghost Walk fun and memorable. In this case, my impromptu speaker, in his seventies, shared his personal experience with a group that spanned many ages. Once he got started, he talked and talked, and many other people came to see what was happening. By the time he concluded and had answered many questions, there were no less than seventy-five people listening in awe.

The story of Lerona took longer than I had expected. I'd stationed myself at the bottom of the stairs to wait for the bulk of my group to come down. The stairs are the only possible exit from the Lodge beyond a knotted rope fire escape. But they never, ever showed up. I sent the remnant of my group off with another Ghost Host and continued to wait for the return of the rest.

It turns out there had been two other Ghost Hosts who had already taken their guests up into the lodge. The lodge holds at least 150 people, so even with my large group, we weren't crowding them.

Shortly into the old-timer's stories of Lerona, the two Ghost Hosts brought their groups down. I greeted them, and off they went to their next stops. None of my folks were with them—I double-checked.

Then another Ghost Host arrived, went up with his group and came back down to await their exit. I questioned him about my group. No, he said. There was nobody else up there but his group. The place was empty when they got to the second floor.

Perplexed, I scanned the streets around again. No one had come out, of that I was sure. Was I worried? Maybe a little. But to be truthful, I was more worried about having disappointed my group than of having lost them. There can be all kinds of trickery on Ghost Walk night. Never once did I envision a headline that read, "Scores of Ghost Walkers Disappear in Masonic Lodge."

Then, to my surprise, two blocks away I saw a solitary man whom I knew to have been in my missing group. He was waving and calling. I walked quickly in his direction, as he was coming toward me.

"There you are," he said. "We wondered where you'd gone."

Where did he come from? With whom had he been on the Ghost Walk? He talked about the rest of the group as if they were still touring. He'd gotten tired and decided to come back to see what was happening downtown.

Thankfully, there was no word in the morning of vanished people, but to this day, I do not know what happened to that group or who took them on the rest of the tour.

ANOTHER GHOST WALK STORY

The second year of the Ghost Walk, I was walking with my group, and we had made the last turn and were ready to see the last couple of sites on the tour. A young man tapped me on the shoulder. "Excuse me," he said, "My great-aunt is on this tour. She was a Hop Princess in 1932." I asked, "Would she like to share some things with us?" and got an affirmative answer together with a big smile.

What a delightful surprise! The tour stopped where it was. I asked the young man to bring his great aunt to the front and put her in a lighted area. "Would you be willing to tell about some of your experiences as a Hop Princess?" I prompted.

In the original Hop Festival, which ran from about 1930 to 1950, a Hop Queen and Court were crowned annually as part of the festivities. Candidates were sponsored by local businesses, and the public voted on their choice for queen. Having businesses nominate candidates was a common practice for many contests in rural communities. And, it seemed, the stronger or more influential the nominating group, the more likely its candidate was to win. The queen and her court ruled until their successors were chosen. No power came with the position, but often winners received discounts from local merchants. Other perks were more varied, such as what happened to our unexpected encounter with a Hop Princess.

She shared such wonderful memories with us. Here is what I recall from that night:

> *Yes, I was a Hop Princess in 1932. I would have been Hop Queen, but the Elks Club sponsored another girl, not me. The Elks Club candidate always got to be queen. I don't know why.*
>
> *In those days, businesses along Main Street were invited to sponsor candidates. One of the girls would be selected queen, and the rest of us would be princesses.*
>
> *But being princess turned out to be OK. As a prize we got some little free things from downtown stores. We had special dresses made to look alike. The best thing was that we got to stay at the dentist's house and sleep on his floor. He had the nicest house in town, right by the river. And he had a motor car and he took us for rides.*
>
> *During the Hop Festival, the royal court was put up on a temporary stage in the Hop Bowl. One morning we were asked to put on our swimsuits, then we were wrapped in hop vines and posed for a group picture.*
>
> *My sister was a Hop Princess in 1937. She didn't get to be queen because she wasn't sponsored by the Elks Club, either.*

A couple details require explanation at this point. Independence has a large park that sits on the bank of the Willamette River. It is a community gathering place and has been for many generations. This was true long before the arrival of the wagon trains. It has a natural bowl shape, sculpted by the many times it flooded during the winter season. In the early days of Independence, it was called the "Hop Bowl" because it was also the place that was naturally the center of community gathering and celebration. Today there is a beautiful amphitheater in the park, taking advantage of its natural bowl shape.

The other point concerns being wrapped in hop vines. Hops are first cousin to a nettle plant, and a significant portion of the population is allergic to hops. Hops are very thorny and have a toxin in the vines and thorns. When this makes contact with the skin of an allergic person, it can raise very uncomfortable and nasty-looking welts. I suspect that a few of the members of that early Hop Court had some unpleasant moments due to their hop-vine experience.

CHAPTER 7

RIVERVIEW PARK

The park is seated in a large, natural semicircular depression. In the early days, it was known as the Hop Bowl. Today, there is a beautiful three-thousand-seat outdoor amphitheatre. A lot of changes have come to this park.

The history of this park is an interesting story in itself. The park is located at the north end of downtown and snuggles up against the Willamette River. The street bordering its south side, C Street, was once the main thoroughfare of Independence. C Street was the original parade route in Independence. Parades began seven blocks away at what is now Pioneer Park and culminated at the river here, at the biggest park in town.

The original users of this park were Native American. Before the arrival of wagon trains and pioneers, this natural bowl and the surrounding swale was a popular camping and trading ground for local tribes. Chief among them were the Kalapuyas. Today the Kalapuyas are part of the Confederated Tribes of Grand Ronde. Members of the Grand Ronde tribes are found in residence all over Polk County, including in Independence.

The *Oregon Encyclopedia* provides this information:

> *Many of the Indians in the Willamette Valley were already well-trained in the American style of agriculture and had integrated their ways of life with that of the new American settlers. "The Twallatty's* [a branch of the Kalapuya] *are, many of them, very good farmers," the April*

26, 1851, Oregonian reported, "and are employed extensively during the harvest season in getting in the crops."

The seasonal harvest for Oregon natives approximated the "seasonal round" of pre-settlement native societies. In the seasonal round, families temporarily moved to important resource areas in an annual cycle. In the process, tribes such as the Kalapuyans harvested and stored camas, seeds, basketry materials, acorns, animals, and fish at specific locations throughout the Willamette Valley.

Natives from the Grand Ronde and Siletz agencies continued to pursue agriculture on the reservations. Many of the men would participate year-round in timber harvesting, while the rest of the family would travel to the hop fields. Native harvesters worked mostly in Independence, near Wheatland Ferry, in Eugene, and in fields near Portland.

Entire families contributed to the harvest, with children allocated smaller containers and shorter hours. Farmers built small shanty towns on their farms, where families occupied rude cabins grouped in ethnically separated "neighborhoods." The farmers held weekly dances, had a general store, showed movies, and provided ice cream for the children.

Today, the Kalapuya (also known as Calapooia or Kalapooia) are part of the Confederated Tribes of the Grand Ronde. According to www.grandronde.org, their traditional homeland is in the Willamette Valley, from the Cascade Mountains to the Coast Range.

Independence Amphitheater. *Courtesy the author.*

The Hop Bowl, which is presently Riverview Park, was an important trading area to the Kalapuya and other tribes. There is a large swale starting four blocks away from the river. An elementary school is at the west end of this swale. In the early days of the school, children regularly found arrowheads on the playground. Once I found an arrowhead among the gravel brought in an alley at mid-swale. A swale is a lowland near a body of water subject to frequent flooding. Native Americans assembled where the community still gathers. Our mayor calls the park the "Living Room of Independence." There may be a cultural memory that infuses the park, because it just feels right as a gathering place.

Starting in the 1930s, any September would find a town full of folks celebrating the end of the hop harvest, and much of the celebration was centered at the park. The Hop Festival was a well-known citywide party. Festivities were particularly pronounced because of the geographical setting of Independence. Less than two miles away was Monmouth, the quiet university town that was dry—no alcohol at all—for many years. Independence had built a reputation as a party town, enhanced by its dry environs. People who knew how to party anyway really pulled out the stops for Hop Festival!

Riverview Park was originally dubbed the Hop Bowl. The swale and bowl-shaped park continued as a natural gathering place. For quite a while, it was the sporting center of Independence, hosting basketball and baseball. Independence had a banner year in sports in 1937. The excitement was palpable as folks came to see the one-season-wonder, the Hopster Hoopsters. This hometown basketball team had an undefeated—and unscored—championship season. Games were played right here in the Hop Bowl. The basketball team is the darling of the community, and with good reason. What sporting prowess!

In 1959, the Hop Bowl was full of covered wagons, campfires, horses and sounds of camaraderie. This was the On to Oregon Cavalcade, an event organized to celebrate one hundred years of Oregon statehood. A fleet of covered wagons reenacted the trek from Independence, Missouri, to Independence, Oregon. Once at the Hop Bowl, they had reached their destination and were celebrating arrival at the "promised land."

The statehood centennial was celebrated all across Oregon. In 1959, I was a very small child living with my family in Pendleton. A challenge had been issued to Oregon men to grow beards in honor of the centennial. My father's facial hair was sparse, and his beard looked more beatnik than pioneer. To my young eyes, it was a scary sight!

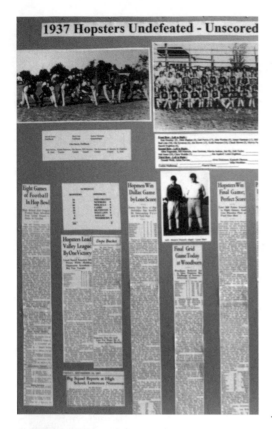

Left: Undefeated Hopster Hoopsters. *Courtesy Heritage Museum/photo by author.*

Below: Load of hops. *Vintage postcard found on Flikr.*

As an adult, I was given some of my grandmother's personal memorabilia. Included was a CD that had been made of her home movies. One nostalgic afternoon, I watched the entire CD. Included was footage of Pendleton's Westward, Ho! parade, associated with the Round-Up celebrations. The On to Oregon Cavalcade was part of the parade.

There is a delightful story about how Riverview Park became a distinct entity beyond just the "Hop Bowl." This occurred in the mid-1960s.

Dee Taylor, a local businessman and town dignitary, owned one of the buildings we'll visit near the end of the Ghost Walk. It is Mr. Taylor who is credited with having made this space an "official" park. Dee Taylor loved Independence, particularly its downtown. He was a staunch supporter of making the traditional gathering space in Independence into a bona fide park. The business of making the park official had begun, but Dee was disgusted with the time it was taking for local authorities to agree and move the process forward. Local lore says that Dee and a couple of his friends, of the same mind about park-building, went out in the middle of the night and did some unplanned landscaping. They plowed an area at the top of the park for plantings, put in some tasteful bushes and declared it a park.

The next morning, city officials were surprised to see the clandestine improvements. They were apparently motivated to get going, because it was just a short time later that Riverview Park came (legally) to be. Several years later, Dee's buddies had a plaque made up crediting him with creation of the park. That plaque, commemorating Dee Taylor's midnight achievement, is still in place within the architecture of the amphitheater.

Fast-forward to 2004. Now we are looking at stark, bare ground in this natural depression. The city council approved upgrades to the park, including a fortuitous and money-saving agreement with the National Guard, which agreed to host training exercises that would accomplish grading and pre-finishing the ground at the park. In 2004, the National Guard's mission was completed. After three years, the park space was ready for amphitheater-building to begin.

The work would have been done sooner, except the National Guard was pulled off this domestic project to fight horrific forest fires. Return to the project could have been delayed, perhaps indefinitely, if not for a serendipitous phone call.

Mayor John McArdle knew that after a year's absence, the amphitheater project could be pushed into the background. In order to keep the work on the National Guard's current to-do list, the mayor made a call to a number he'd been given. A military-trained voice answered the phone, and the Mayor launched into his plea for continuance of the amphitheater work. When he had made his pitch, there was a slight pause, after which the military man asked how McArdle had gotten this number. John explained it was an "as needed" contact number. "Well, son," said the voice, "you've reached the Pentagon." John was in fact talking to a multi-starred general stationed in Washington, D.C. "Tell me more." So John told him more.

The next call came from a major, the officer in charge of the local project. He checked in with the mayor to schedule work for the upcoming season. The major was perplexed. He wasn't sure how or why, but the amphitheater project had ended up as the number one priority for the National Guard nationwide.

CHAPTER 8

STORIES FROM RIVERVIEW PARK

The park is part of a swale that goes from higher ground near the elementary school and culminates in a broad bowl at the river's edge. Regular floods have helped to carve the shape. They have also left higher ground at the top of the park, in the form of a wide plaza shape. This upper portion is now incorporated into the park. In past years, it was a seat of commercial enterprise. The premier business at park top for many years was a livery stable, long gone. A livery stable of some sort was a fixture in Independence, itself a seat of transportation.

Transportation was key to much of early Independence. Besides the livery stable, Independence had a ferry, steamboats and riverboats, two stagecoach companies and a bustling rail business. Monmouth, the neighbor to the west, was built as a separatist community and in its early days did not encourage large groups of visitors, so the transportation industry settled itself in Independence. The top of the park was the area from which departure was often arranged. It was the logical location for the livery stable.

We do not of know any spectral stories (yet) that came from these places of transportation. But stories involving disaster in the form of fire and flood—that's different.

This street-level commercial area consisted mostly of wood buildings. Although out of the worst of the flood zone, these early buildings were not immune to fire.

Disastrous fire in commercial wooden structures is part of many cities' history, from London to Chicago. Independence, on a smaller scale, was

Taylor's Livery Stable at the corner of Main and B Streets, 1959. *Courtesy Heritage Museum.*

no different. Local history includes a broad record of burned buildings. More than once, businesses on Main Street, including at the top of the park, were swept away by fire. There is a recurrent story about hearing— even recording—an unseen someone shout, "Fire! Fire!" in downtown buildings on Main Street. Apparently the memory of conflagration lingers in downtown.

In Independence, there are two large celebrations that occur downtown and include the Hop Bowl and the river. The first, a natural with the town name, happens around the Fourth of July. Independence celebrates national independence with flair. On the park, the fourth will be filled with more than twenty thousand visitors who come to see some pretty spectacular fireworks. In September, the Independence Hop and Heritage Festival, starting with the Ghost Walk, is the big downtown event. Though they are completely separate events, many folks work on both activities, so there is charitable sharing of ideas and advertising.

From right here at the top of the park, a modern story begs to be told. It was the day before Independence Day. The love of fireworks is so acute here that we have them two nights. The "big one" is on July 4. The second show is called "Hometown Fireworks." It's a little smaller than the big one but not as well announced. It is for us locals to enjoy.

On Hometown Fireworks night, a special thing had been planned. A young lady named Joy was going to receive a marriage proposal. Her fiancé-to-be was a pyrotechnician who worked on the seasonal shows. He had been building a giant board to spell out—in fireworks—just the right message for Joy.

The fireworks were about to start. There's often a ground show that is the prelude to the rocket launches, and tonight was no different. Then the board began to light up. It read:

JOY I ♥ U

WILLY

The crowd was delighted, saying, "Awww" and clapping, but I was perplexed. I knew Joy, and her intended was *not* named Willy!

Suddenly, a figure ran to the board with a torch. He touched it to the space just beyond the "Y" in Willy. And the message lit up all the way:

JOY I ♥ U

WILL YOU MARRY ME

More applause from the crowd erupted. I got it now. There was just a break in the fuse line.

This is a story that is retold often. Few people know the inside scoop, but even without that knowledge, it's a charming tale.

CHAPTER 9

TOP OF THE PARK AND
C STREET CORNER

The corner of Main and C Streets is the site of a veterans' memorial. This lovely space was created by a collaboration of AmVets, the American Legion and the City of Independence.

But before there were memorials and collaborations, there was another structure at this site. It was the first multiuse building in Independence. Now we think of multiuse defining a place where businesses and services, perhaps even dwellers, come together. But this was not the case for the first multiuse building. It was one structure that simply changed its use as needed. Local lore has it that use changed nearly every day of the week.

Picture this, on a summer week in the 1870s or 1880s:

Sunday morning: Folks are coming from around the area to hear this morning's sermon by a well-liked pastor. Church services can be long, but at least a cool breeze is coming in off the river. And ladies have brought food for after the service. When the pastor gets hungry enough, he'll stop talking.

Monday morning: The kids are coming to school at this building. It houses all the grades and probably has but one teacher. The space is filled with the accoutrements of teaching. School sessions are held most weekdays, as long as the teacher is healthy, the weather is good and children aren't needed at home to help with the important stuff.

Friday night: Well, things got a little rowdy in town tonight. Two young guys were fighting in the street after having a few drinks. They were probably arguing over some girl. It got way too serious when one of them drew a gun and started firing in the air. The police came and dragged them both here.

There are some sturdy rings in the wall, great for chaining somebody to until they cool off. They'll stay here overnight, and the police will unlock them in the morning. It's not a fancy jail, but it serves us OK.

Saturday night: It's the shank of harvest, a rough day, and it makes a worker thirsty. Good thing the facilities of a bar are here, too. It's open most nights of the week, except Sunday, of course. Sometimes it's so full that guys have to sit on little kids' school desks. But that's not a problem, as long as the spirits are flowing.

From a vantage point at the corner of Main and C Streets, we can see east and west, up and down C Street. East, you can look out over the river, and west, the view stretches several blocks back. Though it is plain where Main Street is today, running parallel to the river, at one time C Street was the main thoroughfare through Independence.

The steamboat *Canemah* was in the first wave of powered river travel to land at Independence. It wasn't until 1851 that the Willamette saw any type of boat that was not powered by man. But this new power could be dangerous, too. The *Canemah* was destroyed by an explosion. Its boiler blew up and took some of the crew with it.

On Main Street, there are two steeples. The one in the foreground is on the Cooper Building; in the background is the Hirshberger Building. These served as navigation points for the steamboat captains searching for a safe landing. For the *Canemah*, which carried mail to Independence for many of the very earliest years of the town, it suffered a fate not uncommon to steam vessels. In 1853, its boiler exploded, killing one passenger. The boat was refitted and returned to service, until it was dismantled in 1858.

The boat *Independence* landed at the town dock. At the eastern base of the street was first a steamship dock and then a ferry landing. Shown in the accompanying photograph is the ferry letting off cars at the base of C Street, constructed to be a ferry landing. Many travelers were brought by wagon or truck to the ferry landing on the east side of the river. They caught the ferry into town and walked from there. Steamships also frequented this dock. *Courtesy Heritage Museum.*

The steeples of Main Street were valuable landmarks to river traffic as navigation points. *Courtesy Heritage Museum.*

As mentioned earlier, transportation was a foundation industry in Independence. The river was a prime means of moving goods, workers and mail.

From this same area comes a persistent story, told since the 1950s. The story involves a young Hispanic mother and her missing son. The son was presumably lost to the river, and the mother—or her spirit—returns often to the riverbank to call for her missing child. A young boy out on his paper route has heard the mother calling but saw no one. It is said that in the early morning or the late evening, when things are quiet at the river, the mother can be heard crying and calling out her child's name.

During one Ghost Walk, a Hispanic friend heard me tell this short story. She told me later that the story of the mother crying and calling for her lost child is far older. She thought the story must have been brought by immigrants from Mexico. If it has roots in truth or not, it is certainly an effective teaching tale for youngsters about the dangers around rivers and why children should stay near and obey their parents. I cannot explain how a local paperboy heard the woman from an imported Mexican tale while walking on the banks of an Independence river.

Of interesting note is this Mexican ghost story that appears many places under the title "La Llorona" (the crying woman). The following version, retold by S.E. Schlosser, comes from a website devoted to American folklore, americanfolklore.net:

> *Once a Spanish soldier married a beautiful native woman and they had two children whom the soldier loved very much. However, the soldier came from a rich family. His parents and relations disapproved of his wife and threatened to disown him unless he married a Spanish woman. Not wishing to lose his inheritance, the soldier put away his native wife and sent for a bride from Spain.*

The soldier's wife was filled with a terrible, jealous rage. To revenge herself against her unfaithful husband, she drowned their two children in the river. The soldier was horrified when he heard what she had done, and tried to have her arrested. But his wife, driven insane by rage, jealousy, and guilt, escaped into the wilds. She roamed through the land, searching the waterways for her children. But she could not find them. Finally, in agony of body and mind, she drowned herself in the river too.

But the woman's spirit could not escape to heaven because of the weight of her terrible crime. And so La Llorona, the Wailing Woman, spirit still wanders the earth, wailing in guilt and grief. She is condemned forever to search in vain for her children. But she will never find them, for they are no more.

The river has always been an attractive place for kids and adults to come and swim. But it can be a wicked river in some moods, and there is a long history of drownings, often reaching double digits in a single summer. In the mid-twentieth century, the Independence Swimming Pool was built because these tragic losses occurred with unbearable regularity. The city fathers took action and built a safer place for everyone to swim.

To the west is a one-way corridor edged by businesses. Today this portion of the street has the distinction of being filled with female-owned and/or female-run businesses. But in the days of this street being the main thoroughfare in town, it looked quite different. In those days, C Street from Main to Second boasted a solid block of saloons. As has been said before, a party-loving town—work hard and play hard—described Independence in the early days.

The Main Street of today runs parallel to the Willamette River. It is known as Oregon Highway 51 until it reaches downtown and becomes Main. Remember the two towns that were founded, one by Thorpe to the north and one by Hill to the south? In the early days, the portion of street that became north Main, running through Thorpe's area, had a different title. It was called Indian Burial Mounds Street. I can surmise why the street was named so and hope that proper respect was exercised during the period of road building.

When the hop industry was in full swing, this was a well-used area. Hops were central for a century or more in the area, but they certainly ruled in the years from 1900 to 1940.

Hops, by their nature, take a long time to go from rootstock to hop bale. There is no money realized by the grower until the bales are sold. But the workers are needed from the first time green pokes from the rootstock. This disconnect was handled by local hop growers through the vehicle of scrip. Workers were paid during the growing and harvesting season in scrip—a form of IOU—and there was a standing agreement with local merchants to accept the scrip as money. All season long, workers traded in town using scrip. At the end of the harvest, merchants gathered up their scrip, visited the various hop farms and redeemed the IOUs for money growers had made from the ultimate sale of the hop bales.

Scrip was legal tender from bank to bar. All bars were within easy walking distance of the ferry landing, for downtown was compact then, focused into four blocks.

One other historic fact that shows the importance of C Street to early Independence is that it was the town's official parade route. Parades began seven blocks away, where they formed and staged at a local park. The parade then moved from formation to finish at the Hop Bowl/Riverview Park. This was the traditional route for all local parades.

CHAPTER 10

FIRST NATIONAL BANK

O n the southeast corner of C Street is a quaint building left untouched by fire or demolition. It was built originally as a First National Bank building in 1885. It was the first bank in Independence and, according to the City of Independence website, was said to be "one of the most compact and neatly furnished and equipped office buildings in the state, furnished with the latest improved chronometer lock safe, and a fine large fire proof vault which has the best doors of any deposit vault in the valley."

This building has also served as a tavern—quite a step down from a bank. From 1907 to 1913, it was the U.S. Post Office. It has also housed Charbonneau's Meat and Grocery store, an import shop, a travel agency, a children's resale shop, a candy store and a café.

The City of Independence has a fine section on their website covering local history. Data comes from several sources, including the Heritage Museum and the early local publications, copies of which are housed at the Independence Public Library, and from the application made by the City of Independence for all of downtown to be named a historic district. That application was a success, and as a result, there is a strong preservation group locally. Historic information comes from this website, unless otherwise noted. For more detailed information on any of these buildings, visit www.ci.independence.or.us, and click the "history" button. Most of the historic building information is drawn from this site, and it will be noted if there is another source.

Corner of Main Street and C Street in the early days. *Courtesy Heritage Museum.*

Mayor's home on Monmouth Street. *Courtesy the author.*

There was an obscure, and unfortunately now lost, photo from 1912 that showed this building. Snuggled to the back of it was a temporary lean-to structure. The little structure had a sign on it that read, "the Lerandra Brother's Show." Today we don't know who the Lerandra brothers were, nor do we know what kind of show they put on. It would have been during the time that the building housed the U.S. Post Office. We don't believe the Lerandas were selling stamps…

A picture recently surfaced that might explain some of the mystery. A circus came through town from time to time. In the picture, the First National Bank building is sporting an extension marked "Sells-Floto Circus."

The current business owner in this building, on Ghost Walk night, tells about the many strange bumps and squeaks heard from inside the building, especially after the sun goes down. One of the most common downtown ghostly happenings occurs here. The front door is heard to open, as if a customer has come in. The owner comes to greet them, but no one (visible) is there.

Perhaps doors are a common vehicle for communication among the unseen population. This story comes from Patty Nevue, wife of Mayor John McArdle, concerning a house seven blocks away from downtown. The house was built by the owner of the Independence Creamery and is one of the most elegant houses in town. The Creamery, itself once on south Main Street, was a business central to Independence until it burned down.

Nevue says:

> *There have always been odd sounds and temperature variances in our house. Nothing has ever really scared me. But recently something has been happening that has made me very sad.*
>
> *Our son moved off to college, and I think the house has been missing him. The door to his room opens and closes spontaneously. This happens most often when our son would have come home from school after football practice. It has been over a year now, and the house must still be lamenting his departure.*

CHAPTER 11
SOUTH MAIN STREET SHOPS

OVENBIRD BAKERY

Ovenbird Bakery is in a small brick building slid in next to the First National Bank building on the corner. The space has housed a variety of small businesses. The most recent renovation, completed two years ago to prepare for the bakery, revealed an unusual space.

Out of view from the street, there is a wall that had a red substance on it. The new proprietors expected to simply paint over the wall, and they did. Again, and again and again. The red substance, itself a little viscous, kept bleeding through.

Though we have no evidence, empirical or anecdotal, of evil or malicious spirits, whatever inhabits the space at Ovenbird may encourage instability. Ten years ago, a coffee shop set up operation in the spot. The owner brought in fresh local music and displayed local art. It was a busy place, especially on the evenings with live music. The owner seemed bent on success until one morning, after more than a year of operation, the door was locked. There was a handwritten note with an obscure message about the owner moving to Arizona. Later, the story drifted back to town that the owner was fearful of her downtown neighbor. She said he was stalking her, and she just had to flee. When the same claim was made against the owner by her supposed stalker, the mystery deepened even more.

Next came another coffee shop, much more conservative in nature. Again, the shop made steady progress, becoming quietly prosperous. Then an odd turn again occurred. The shop was locked during one of the busiest weekends of the year, the Fourth of July. A huge crowd is drawn to Independence for its second-to-none fireworks. With it comes the sales that shops welcome. But the shop owner at this location made the sudden decision to close because it was too busy. At the next downtown event, the shop was again closed, never to reopen.

The next store came in. Shortly after open, the proprietor said her husband had lost his job, and suddenly there was more dependence on income from the shop than ever before. The shop catered to a niche market but just couldn't meet the economic needs of the owner's family. They transferred their business to a larger community.

That brings us to the time of the bakery, the current business in the building at the time of this writing. The bakery was a hit from the start. But it wasn't long before disagreements between the partners began. In less than a year, the partnership of three turned into a two-against-one rivalry. The bakery is doing fine, but the spirit of disruption is still in play.

223 SOUTH MAIN STREET

Next to the bakery is a little shop that was once two shops. There is a bathroom with two doors so that each shop/office owner had access to the facilities. There is a double glass door in front that allowed individual access. The wall dividing the spaces, though, is long gone.

This building has been home to many businesses, the most recent being a shoe shop, mountaineering supply, insurance office, antique store, linen shop, youth business academy, secondhand shop and today's business, an artisan co-op.

The stories that come from this shop are more modern, though the space doesn't seem to cotton to modern electronics. Computers have turned off inadvertently; printers work and then don't. But it is the radio that appears to take on a mind of its own. When a station is tuned in that plays country music, the radio goes off or will have so much static that it must be turned off. When the station is changed, the reception is fine. Find another country station, same problem, same solution.

A dapper older man dressed in clothing from the late 1800s has been seen a couple times in the store. Once he was there-and-not-there in the corner of a store, and the other time he was seen waiting at the counter, though briefly.

The door in this establishment behaves as many do on Main Street. Countless times the door was heard to open, and when staff hopped up to see who was there, the store was empty. Management put bells on the door to allow for a more distinctive sound when it was opened in the event that the door was being jiggled or rattled when heavy traffic went by. But the bells didn't deter the mysterious sound of a door opening. The bells would sound as they were supposed to, the door was heard to open with its customary noises and still nobody was there.

Finally, a truly odd thing happened. A group of staff members were seated on the floor organizing merchandise. One young woman was positioned with her back to the bathroom. On a shelf just outside the bathroom, and a little around the corner from where staff were sitting, was a mug with metal teaspoons in it. Without warning, a spoon came sailing out of the bathroom alcove and landed right behind the young woman. This "trick" was witnessed by several people.

A Split Café

Here is the case of a building with two parts, two owners, but one business. Since it was built in 1916, the left portion of the building was a barbershop under various owners and remained as such for many years. The taller right side was built in 1910. Evidence shows that a meat market was there first. Other businesses came and went, but use as a meat market was recurrent through the building's history, up to at least 1950.

When the buildings were joined by opening the adjoining wall, it became attractive as a restaurant site. First came Nedrey's, then Hazel's, Big Jim's and now Andy's. Andy's has been *the* local hangout in Independence. It serves meals for the workingman—in workingman portions—and is an important point of information exchange. It is not unusual for someone on one side of the restaurant to ask a question and shortly have it answered by someone else many tables away. Andy's is a hub!

For most of the ghostly stories, we go back to the days of the meat market. The building on the right side has a basement under it. In the basement,

235 South Main Street. *Courtesy the author.*

below the meat market, are still two hooks and pulleys, two big metal basins with wide drains and a small door at mid-wall height. The practice was to bring a fresh carcass into the basement and hang it by a hook over a metal basin. The carcass was skinned and gutted there. Unusable parts went down the drain, which exited directly to the river. These were the days before enlightened environmentalism.

The now dressed carcass was moved to a spot over the second drain. There cuts of meat were sliced off. The small door in the wall was opened. Inside was a dumbwaiter. The choice cuts were placed inside for delivery to the meat market floor above.

Owners of the restaurant held a split opinion about ghostly activity in the building. He said nothing was going on, but she said that's not so. She does not like the basement or being in the store after dark. She saw things, heard things and has friends who back up her claims. The owner was not specific about the incidents, beyond ghostly sounds, catching action out of the corner of an eye or feeling just generally creepy when in the basement. Is the butcher still in residence, or is it some of the many animals who were prepared for consumption?

Time went by and took Andy's Café to another location. The new tenants work with electronics, and ghostly stories are pouring out of the building now. Those in the know, spectrally, say that ghosts are drawn to residual power sources and latent electricity. Batteries and power supplies are a favorite. The shop owner says in the morning he often finds his stash of used power supply units scattered about, as if hands had dug through the collection, tossing aside what's useless, looking for that certain spark.

CHAPTER 12

MURAL ON MAIN AND THE "W" BUILDING

Not all of the stories on the Ghost Walk are spectral or mysterious. Some are quite humorous.

Today in the center of the middle block on the west side of Main Street there is a mural by well-known and respected artist Mel Blanchard. Originally an open space between two buildings on ground not well built-up to receive a structure, the space is now designated a "pocket park." In 1986, the mural was painted and the park was made official on the books. Folks assume it was a means to cover an unsightly area.

There is a classic anecdotal tale that took place at this site, before the mural and the park came into being, and when the opening with its unpleasant view still existed. In the 1970s, there was a young thief who had his eye on a jewelry store, which was then located across the street from the site of the present-day mural. At that time, pre-mural, there was an open space with a short split-rail fence edging the back of the sidewalk.

Our thief crafted a plan. He would rob the jewelry store, bag up his loot and then run for the river using the handy break in the sidewalk for easy access. He brought two of his friends into the plan, whose job would be to wait for him in a getaway boat. The friends agreed, and the plan was set.

On the day of the robbery, things started so well. The thief robbed the store (check). The bag he'd brought to gather the booty was full and easy to carry (check). It was going too well. He ran across the street and, speeding

Mural on Main Street, painted by Mel Blanchard, muralist. *Courtesy Dan Haneckow.*

for the getaway boat, vaulted the short fence. On his way over the fence, he must have at last realized his mistake.

Blackberry bushes filled his landing place. Many feet wide, and several feet deep, they waited. He landed right in the brambles and became well and truly stuck. By then, the jewelry storeowner had called the police and witnessed the escape. The police came and called the fire department. The firemen took their time cutting the young thief out of his thorny trap. Meanwhile, his friends and the getaway boat departed quietly.

THE "W" BUILDING

South of the mural on Main, there is a building, erected in 1915, decorated with a "W." The meaning of the initial is unclear. But we do know that the first tenant was a tavern. The location remained a tavern until the early 1990s. I became familiar with this building when we moved to town. On the very first weekend of our residence in Independence, I went for a stroll downtown. I knew there'd been some police activity the night before, but I was unprepared for what met me. This building, at 265 South Main Street, was at that time Kay's Tap Room, a bar with a bad reputation. On this day, the entryway was blocked off with crime scene tape. On the sidewalk there

The "W" Building hosted many a spirited drinker in its day. *Courtesy the author.*

was an honest-to-goodness chalk outline. It seems that, during the course of a police sting, there had been a fatal stabbing. The tavern was a crime scene and was closed for business until cleared by law enforcement.

At the time, it made me feel so warm and confident about choosing Independence as a place to live!

Later, when it was reopened, Kay's Taproom and another bar up the street were again closed down by a large sting operation. Each place had been caught selling alcohol to minors and dispensing recreational drugs from behind the bar.

Today a martial arts studio is in the building. But one wooden wall on the south side has been preserved from tavern days. Lots of names and words are carved into the wood, many of them recognizable to locals.

This location is surely haunted by a wealth of lingering angst and memories. Recently I spoke to the policeman who had drawn the chalk outline in front of the building on the night of the stabbing. He refrained from giving any details, except to say, "Bad, bad place. We all hated going in there." There must be layers upon layers of uncomfortable history. Perhaps the martial arts studio is doing its part to exorcise the worst of the memories.

CHAPTER 13

ELK'S LODGE

Independence Elks Lodge No. 1950 was chartered in March of 1955. It wasn't long after that the organization decided to purchase the Main Street property, which previously housed a grocery store and a J.C. Penney, said Ed Pomeroy, a member from Monmouth.

The lodge was gutted by a three-alarm fire that broke out in a corner of the main dining room the morning of March 24, 1979. Insurance money and loans were used to rebuild the property in 1980, while the Elks also incorporated the old Isis Theater next door into part of their headquarters.
—Craig Coleman, Itemizer-Observer

Fire appears again. Maybe it was this building that prompted the call of "Fire, Fire!" heard on the paranormal investigator's tape.

When the Isis Theater was open, downtown Independence bustled with all types of retail outlets, such as J.C. Penney, Sears and the like. We presume that it must have been more of a chore getting to the big town of Salem in those days. When commuting became the norm, as did shopping in the city, the big retailers closed their small-town sites.

This building, the restructuring of two previous buildings, has produced some interesting spectral evidence. But first, there is a curious tale about something more mundane: a spider's web.

In a recessed area of the building, a spider web was discovered. It had been long vacated, but it remained strong and extensive. Caught still in the web was the skeleton of a small bird. This points to a rather large spider that

Left: Independence Elk's Lodge. *Courtesy the author.*

Below: Fire! Elk's Lodge burns, 1979. *Photograph by Ed Pomeroy. Courtesy* Itemizer Observer.

could spin a web to catch (and possibly eat) a bird. The bird—in desiccated form—still exists. Apparently the Elks were so impressed by the vigor of the spider that they cemented the remains of the bird in place, half in and half out of the wall, in tribute. It is still there today.

The Elks Club members have conducted some investigations of their own. They have what they say are genuine photos of ghosts, taken with a computer whose camera was set to record anything that came in its field of vision. One of the most recent pictures captured is not a human spirit. The image of a horse's head is clearly depicted as one of the beings that came by to have its picture taken. Of the other ghostly pictures, some are stills, like the horse head, and some are blurry and elongated, as if they just sped by on the way to somewhere else. After talking to folks who investigate haunted sites, I have learned that animal sightings are quite rare. That must mean the appearance of a discmbodicd hcad of an animal is especially unique.

It is fascinating to contemplate the unusually successful meeting of the old (spirits) and new (computers). We have seen the same fortunate collaboration at our next stop, the Masonic lodge building.

CHAPTER 14

THE MASONIC LODGE BUILDING

The official name of the Independence Masonic lodge is the Lyon Lodge No. 29 of the Ancient Free and Accepted Masons. It is the second-oldest fraternal organization in Polk County. The initial meeting of the lodge was held in other quarters in 1859, and the building is named after its first Worshipful Master, Lemuel Lyon. He was a dry good dealer who founded other lodges in Oregon and California.

The building was constructed in three phases in 1892, 1898 and 1914. The entire top floor is the lodge area. The bottom floor houses three businesses. A basement is under it all.

DOWNSTAIRS

For over one hundred years, a hardware store of some type occupied the first floor, beginning in 1902 with an agricultural implements store. Today, the space has been divided into three retail spaces, currently occupied by a pizza parlor, a used bookstore and a hair salon.

When the hardware store was in operation—as it was for the first Ghost Walk—the owner had lots of stories to share. One of his favorites occurred in the basement. The owner was downstairs cutting pipe, and something tapped him on the shoulder. He looked quickly over his shoulder, saw no person there and continued his work. He was tapped again. This time, he

Masonic Lodge. *Courtesy the author.*

took a longer look. It was not a hand that had tapped him—it was a length of pipe, and it hung there, levitating in air, completely unsupported, ready to tap again. The owner decided that if this was ghostly work, it was certainly a mischievous ghost who occupied the basement.

The hardware store moved out, and things were quiet, but only for a while. Today, stories are being told again about happenings in the lower levels of the building.

One already common phenomenon is the door that opens to nobody. There is a bell on this door, too, one that is tripped when the door is opened. It rings frequently when the door stays shut.

Footsteps are regularly heard when no one is visible to cause them. Owners say there is a frequent "not alone" feeling in many areas, especially in a new back room recently remodeled and opened for public use.

A singular event happens at least once a month in the bathrooms: photos are turned to be hanging upside down. About every thirty days, the pictures have to be re-hung. This activity has made owners wonder if it is the prankster up from the basement making his opinion known about the artwork.

Another story has recently come to light. In the early 1970s, there was just one woman on the local police force. She caught a call one night about a break-in down at the hardware store. A tip had been called in that two guys were breaking into the basement entrance of the store, which was around the back.

When the officer arrived, she found the basement door ajar. Quietly, she went down the steps and at the first landing met a silent man dressed in work clothes. He was quietly pointing to a specific section of the basement. She nodded her thanks to the man and followed his direction. Right where he'd pointed, she found the two who'd broken in.

The officer made the collar and, on her way back out and up the stairs, looked for the man who had given her such clear direction. But he was nowhere around. Later at the station, she described her quiet helper. Several of the other officers confirmed the existence of a ghost of the basement who appeared pretty regularly. He was not something to be feared. He did help out and enjoyed a prank from time to time as well.

There is more to the story, but a caution first is needed because it comes from a time before current political awareness. And it has to do with one female police officer on a force otherwise male. When the call came in over the radio, it sounded like this: "Dickless Tracy, break-in at the hardware store!"

Stories have not been reported from the bookstore or the hair salon—at least, not yet.

Upstairs

Though there had not been an official "haunted" history kept by the lodge, when the Ghost Walk started, stories began to emerge. Once again, footsteps in uninhabited areas and doors opening without anyone coming in are a recurrent theme at the lodge building. But it certainly doesn't stop there. Here is a reiteration of stories we have heard since the Ghost Walk began.

One lodge member said he saw a head "popping out" of a wall, as if the person had leaned in to quietly observe the lodge meeting.

Each group who meets or has met at the lodge has a unique ceremony for initiation and meetings. One evening, a lodge member was attending an installation in the girls' group, Job's Daughters. He reported later that he'd observed a stately figure accompanying the newest initiate from stop to stop during the ceremony. The "person" seemed to be lending a steady influence to the young woman who was feeling very nervous. This phenomenon of a silent companion appears not to be an isolated incident. Reports indicate that all the groups have had unexpected spectral guests.

The lodge has hosted several paranormal investigation groups. One group took EMF readings in the lodge and found them particularly strong in a side room. Following the signal, they were led to an old water heater that had been replaced. It was not connected to anything and was empty of liquids. Yet it pulsed with this odd power. It reminded me, when I heard the story, of the holding tank in the *Ghostbusters* movie. The paranormal group planned to come back and check it out some more. However, a lodge member, who is also a firm skeptic, removed the water heater to the dump.

A different paranormal group set up equipment in the upper part of the lodge building, from which footsteps emanated. Tape recording equipment and cameras were put into place. Each time the tape was set up, the investigator would head down the stairs, only to hear the machine turn off. Back he went to turn it on again. And as he went downstairs, *click*, it was off again. Several frustrating repetitions later, there was finally no *click*. When investigators checked a half-hour later, though, the tape machine was firmly off. Nothing was recorded during that visit.

The camera was handled differently. It ran for the entire period of the investigation, but it didn't pick up anything. Perhaps that's because it was constantly in motion. The lens was stationary when the investigators set it up, but the film revealed that the lens had been swept up and down, side to side, and sometimes it appeared the entire camera had been moved far up and down. There were long stretches of film panning the walls. The only clear-cut result was a very frustrated group of paranormal investigators.

Another group of researchers was much luckier. Maybe that was because one of the members of the group is himself a lodge member. Using a different approach, this group set up a light machine and a tape recorder. Investigators moved from area to area in the main lodge room to conduct "interviews." A question would be asked aloud, and whoever was listening was asked to use the light machine to answer—one blink for yes, two for no. The investigators told lodge members that this method had proved successful in other spots.

A lodge is laid out according to the four directions. The east and west are the first and second-most important positions and north and south less so. Knowing that schematic, investigators progressed from south to north and west to east. In the east, they "met" someone. The conversation went along these lines:

"Are you there?"

Yes. (one blink)

"Are you male?"

No. (two blinks)
"Are you female?"
Yes.
"Are you an adult?"
Yes.
"Were you a leader?"
No.
"Were you a member?"
Yes.
"Did you decide to stay here?"
Yes.
"Are you happy?"
Yes.
"Will you keep staying here?"
Yes.

Many more questions were asked and answered. With only two choices, only simple information can be gathered. But the conclusion drawn by the investigating group was that the entity is female and, though not a leader in the lodge, was a longtime member. She must have been a member of the Eastern Star, the women's organization attached to the Masonic lodge. She may have worked with a youth group, but the answers were too inconclusive to completely determine that. Depending on how long she had been ensconced in the east, she could have witnessed many a meeting, including some of the so-called secret work of the men. What came through clearly was that she enjoyed her position of power and planned to continue "living" right there. She was happy.

One of the hallmarks of this building is the abundance of orbs that show up in photographs—especially digital photography. The first year there was just the one orb that showed up over my head, but now hundreds of orb pictures exist.

The newest occurrence in the Masonic lodge is pretty stunning. One of the new Ghost Hosts, a school superintendent, was leading a group into the lodge for the first time. A young man on the tour had his two-year-old son lifted up onto his shoulders. The superintendent and the young man had been chatting off and on. The little boy was quiet, smiling and wide-eyed. As they went up the stairs into the lodge, the boy began a quiet chatter, as two-year-olds will do. The father hushed him a couple of times. The baby talk continued as they were escorted into the main lodge room. The host on site began his talk, and the little boy kept talking. The host took a long pause, and the father said, "Shhh" again, trying to quiet his son. Instead, the boy raised himself a little higher on dad's shoulders, pointed to an open and empty area behind the host, and said clearly, "Who's she?" Nobody was there. The superintendent, who'd been leaning toward skepticism, was aghast. It was another perfect Ghost Walk moment.

CHAPTER 15

THE HIRSHBERG BUILDING

This is the Hirshberg Building. It was constructed in 1891 by the firm of Jackson and Hutchin for a total cost of $12,000. The building, located in Henry Hill's Town Independence, is a fine example of an Italian-style commercial building, designed by architect, Walter D. Pugh. Since this building has been a bank since it was first built, and it still is a bank, it is believed to be the oldest continually operating bank in Polk County, Oregon.
—*enhanced excerpts from a pamphlet available at Sterling Bank, current tenant in the Hirschberg Building*

Prominently situated at the intersection of Main and Monmouth Streets, the Hirshberg Building is an important visual landmark, anchoring the south end of the town's historic commercial core. The stately tower of the bank balances the more elegant tower of the Queen Anne–style Cooper Building one block north. *(Remember the two towers used for navigation?)*

Around 1866, Herman "Joe" Hirshberg organized the Independence City Bank. In 1889, stock was issued and the name was changed to Independence National Bank. About that time, it evidently merged with the older First National Bank of Independence. And First National Bank of Independence opened its doors at Monmouth and Main.

The bank conducts its business on the ground floor. The second floor, though, is more of a time capsule. One area, presumably a foyer or waiting area, has been turned into a break room for employees. Beyond the open area, a hallway extends, with smaller rooms to the right and left.

Hirshberg Building on Main and Monmouth Streets has been a bank since the day it opened. *Courtesy Dan Haneckow.*

One of the rooms still has an attorney's name, printed on a translucent glass door in gold leaf. This area is left untouched, except for a few corners used for storage.

Even after several discussions, the branch manager claims there are no ghostly stories associated with this building. She will allow that there are "odd" things that happen from time to time, but nothing more.

Some of her employees, who are loath to enter the upper realms, disagree. In private conversations, they tell about cold spots and feeling like they're being watched. Many of them refuse to enter the break room.

On Ghost Walk night, an unusual thing does happen: the bank is opened to the public after hours. The manager and her staff take guests on a complete tour of the bank (sans vault). It is one of the popular stops on the walk.

I just met a former occupant of the Hirschberg Building. As a young man he had kept an office upstairs in that very building. When I asked whether he knew of any ghostly occurrences, he replied with a quick, "Oh, yes!" When he had his office there, it was common to walk through cold spots, hear screams and eavesdrop on conversations between speakers who weren't visible. Has the activity calmed down with the coming of a bank? Do the spirits feel more secure? Or are they just integrating into the overall spirit of Independence, which leans more toward fun and away from fear?

Another interesting fact that has turned up concerns activity in second-story downtown. The term "upstairs offices" is a colloquialism. It is the polite way to reference a prostitute's boudoir. Yes, in this bank, there is a door with an attorney's name in gold leaf. But other doors are not marked.

The upper level of downtown was an active place. Today it is a mix of vacant spaces, storage and the occasional residence. But in the past, it was filled with whole different spirit of—fun?

CHAPTER 16

INDEPENDENCE AND HOPS

Independence was once the "Hop Capital of the World." The hop crop and harvest was at one time the dominant feature in the lives and landscapes of Independence. It is important to share some hop history here. Hops were the common thread—vine?—from the past to the present. Hop farming was a way of life for early natives and modern farmers. In the summer, the vines begin to creep up their strings. More and more acres are turning back to hops, as we escalate our enjoyment of subtly flavored beers.

During the months it takes to go from bud to harvest of hops, a large number of agricultural workers are needed to handle the crop. They would live in temporary communities erected by the hop growers.

The following are excerpts from an article by Peter A. Kopp in the *Oregon Encyclopedia*:

> *Early hop production in Oregon occurred on small family farms with typically less than twenty acres dedicated to the crop. In most instances, families grew hops as their sole cash crop, and local families or regional Indians provided the necessary labor for harvest in late August and September.*
>
> *From 1905 to 1915, Oregon held the distinction as the nation's largest hop producer…and by the 1930s (following the repeal of Prohibition), the state's hop growers expanded production to include over 20,000 acres of hops for a number of years…Independence in Polk County was known as the "Hop Center of the World."*

The increase in production required thousands of new seasonal laborers to harvest the crop. Growers advertised in newspapers to recruit urban families and provided cabins or tents, water, and other necessities for the hop-pickers. Many of the operations included entertainment, such as music and campfires, which added to a general festive atmosphere across Oregon during hop harvest season. Pickers enjoyed decent wages and a retreat from the city.

Hop growers provided tents, cabins, etc., for the workers. In the years before World War II, these became small cities at the hop farms. They often had an internal governing structure, even electing a sheriff or law officer for the group.

The hop farm communities entered into spirited competitions with each other, especially in the post-harvest parties. Townspeople had favorites and joined in the fun, at least by cheering for their chosen group. Horse racing in Independence became a serious sport, and lots of money changed hands when a good race was going on.

Migrant workers from Mexico did not arrive in large groups until after World War II. There was much work to be done, and immigrants would bring their entire family to work in the hop fields. I have friends who, as youngsters, picked hops in Independence.

Migrant laborers did not always have the luxury of getting their children to school, so children were given a form of home schooling as the work was being done. These teaching days are remembered fondly. The adults who experienced that in-the-field education say they didn't just learn the basics they would have gotten in school. They also learned cultural history, some social graces, respect for elders, honor for the family structure and great communication skills.

One friend remembers being impressed by her father's skill in the field. Hops, in the growing process, are trained up on strings. Each year the strings must be replaced, staked into the ground and tied off at the top of the pole. She said her father could stand in the back of an old farm truck, brace himself on a ladder tied into the truck bed and reach out far enough to touch the hop stringers on each side of the row. Workers would hand him up strings from each side. My friend's dad must have been ambidextrous, because she said he could simultaneously and one-handedly tie off the strings on the left and right side and then move on to the next. I'm sure none of this process would measure up to OSHA standards today. But it was a valuable skill in its day, and one daddy certainly impressed his little girl.

Hop pickers. *Courtesy City of Independence, Heritage Museum.*

Another friend told me about the smaller bags and baskets the children were given to pick their hops into. Adults were given containers that, when completely full, stood over four feet high and were heavy—heavier than a child could carry or even drag along. So smaller people received smaller baskets and bags. Though they were often slower pickers, it gave the children a sense that they could almost keep up with the adult workers. The hop harvest was for everybody, every age.

A REAL HOP YARD

Growing behind the back of the Independence Library is a miniature hop yard. Four sets of poles grow strings of plants. It differs from a real hop yard both in size and in that there are many varietal representatives in this more ornamental yard.

By the time the Ghost Walk occurs, the hop-growing season has peaked. In the big hop yards, the vines have been harvested. But in our tiny hop yard, they are on the string, tied and grown in the original way and ready for guest inspection. Besides being a key ingredient in beer, hops have been used in many other ways. Hops are listed as a curative agent in an 1887 publication, *Kohler's Medicinal Plants*:

The Herb Hop
(Humulus lupulus)

This herb also contains humulone and lupulone, noted for its anti-bacterial qualities which stimulate gastric juice production aiding in the digestion of food. Hops has been noted to help to prevent the formation of new blood vessels, useful as an herbal anti-cancer agent, preventing different cancer types from starting, growing, or spreading.

Hops contains phyto-estrogen which acts like the female hormone estrogen in the body and is now formulated with other herbs in products that are sold for herbal breast enlargement. As a tea, hop flowers have been used as a remedy for cramps, swellings and hardness of the uterus.

This plant has been used for menstrual difficulties for over 2,500 years, with its earliest uses documented during early Roman and Greek history.

Extracts of hop flowers have been used in treating leprosy, pulmonary tuberculosis, and acute bacterial dysentery. A poultice of the leaf and fruit of the Hops plant has been used to remedy "cold" tumors.

A pomade made from lupulin has been used to remedy cancerous ulcerations. Hops are reputed to decrease sexual desire, increase perspiration and are beneficial as a herbal pain reliever, diuretic, nervine and to expel intestinal parasites.

Hops contains the amino acid asparagin, along with poly-phenolic tannins, which make this herb effective in treating boils, bruises, stones in gallbladder, kidney and urinary tract, cystitis, debility, delirium, diarrhea, dyspepsia, fever, fits, hysteria, inflammation, jaundice, neuralgia, rheumatism, earache or toothache.

Since the time of the pharaohs, hops have been grown and used for brewing beer. On the Ghost Walk, we discuss hops' importance to beer. But we also share some lesser-known information. There is quite a lot of interest from our guests about the hop cone itself. "How do they use the hops?" many will ask. So we harvest a few hop cones—indeed, they do look like a miniscule green pinecones—and go through a couple steps.

Take a smell: Hops have a distinct, sharp odor, and some varieties are more "hoppy" than others.

Separate the leaves of the cone: Check out the tiny amounts of yellow pollen in the core of the hop cone. This is what is used to flavor beer. The actual chemical component is called "lupulin."

Look again at the rest of the cone: Unused portions of the hop cone have a use, too. They are processed and used to create the dye for army uniforms—this is the source of "khaki green."

Some more obscure facts: Hops belong to a family that includes two more familiar plant names: nettles and marijuana. Because of their nettle-like properties, hops in raw form cause an allergic reaction in a large percent of the population. The leaf configuration of hops on the vine have a striking similarity to the marijuana plant, even though the growing pattern is completely different. There appears to be a chemical relationship between the two plants as well.

Hops in other products: Hops, especially the oils, are regular ingredients in personal care products, such as lotions and shampoos. In many skin and body-care products, hops are somewhere in the list of ingredients. Hops are also the basis for herbal medications used for relaxation and as sleep aids. Pillows may be stuffed with hops and given to people who have trouble sleeping. Hops can also be brewed into herbal teas to help promote good sleep. This hop brew is also said to be helpful with digestion and is often made a part of the diet for that reason. Some stories go even farther. It is rumored that a pillow filled with hops when slept on by a man causes him to wake up with more virility and stamina. A woman who sleeps on the same pillow might find her breast size increasing.

Visible from our small hop yard is the local cinema. Before it was built, a hop warehouse stood on the site. It was a fixture in Independence for seventy-five years. This is where hops were baled and shipped by rail to buyers. The building stood right next to the railroad tracks. Trains pulled in, and bales of hops were loaded directly from warehouse to boxcar.

The floor of the hop warehouse was tongue and groove, well made with old-growth timber. But there was a second floor about eighteen inches lower than the wooden one. This second floor was made of concrete. A worker was periodically sent into that eighteen-inch space with a whisk broom and pan to gather the pollen that had sifted between the cracks in the wooden floor. That pollen was the golden crop, and none of it would be lost or wasted.

In more modern times, the building was used for another completely unexpected purpose. Before taking down the building, a thorough inspection was made for usable parts. The huge old-growth timber used as beams drew oohs and aahs from builders. But there was one feature that perplexed everyone. There was a trapdoor that led to the under-flooring. When the door was raised, a pentagram was revealed, etched into the concrete. The symbol told the story of many a witchy gathering. The candles at each point had been replaced many times. The onlookers were shocked. The stories of a haunted downtown were common. But witches in the hop warehouse? That was something entirely unknown.

CHAPTER 17
PINK HOUSE CAFÉ

The Pink House Café is itself a curiosity. This building began its life as a structure a block away from here, close to the hop warehouse. People gasp when they find out that the house was purchased in 2009 for just $500. But the modern methods of home moving are expensive, even if the move is a mere block. Some very old-fashioned techniques were applied to fitting the house neatly into its space. Trees were trimmed by hand, and dirt was shaved with a small hand trowel. Inch by inch, the structure was jiggled into position.

We do not know if anything ghostly occurred in the house before its one-block move. But in its current location, once it was opened as a café, it did not take long for things to start happening. Like many other buildings in downtown Independence, footsteps are heard in unoccupied areas, as well as a rhythmic, gentle pounding. One of the owners believes he has identified the sound—a bouncing ball. Once or twice, a little girl has been seen out of the corner of an eye. She is always spotted upstairs in the second story. This young girl is playful, and no bad feelings or happenings have been attributed to her in any way.

There has been a recent report of another unusual experience at the Pink House Café. A friend of mine loves to host tea parties for adults. She puts on tea parties for fundraisers and is quite accomplished at it. She has collected all the best trimmings and is an expert at presentation and a wonderful baker as well. In 2013, she was preparing a tea party in support of breast cancer research. "The Pink Tea" has become an annual go-to event in

Pink House Café. *Courtesy Dan Haneckow.*

Independence. She had been invited to hold her tea in the Pink House Café, and she was delighted. It is a genteel setting, the appropriate environs for a fancy tea party.

At the Pink House, there is dining upstairs and down. My friend went upstairs to do her fancy settings and preparation work. Finished there, she returned to the main floor to dress it up and get it ready for guests. Every place was set with bone china cups and saucers, small serving trays and silver teaspoons.

As she was setting up downstairs, she heard sounds from the second floor: *clink, tinkle, clinkity-clink.* Curious, she stopped and listened. There was silence for a while, then *clink, tinkle, clinkity-clink.* It happened several times. What was making that sound? She couldn't figure out what it could be.

Suddenly, she knew! She was hearing the sound of tea being stirred in an empty cup. A little sugar, perhaps a little cream and then stir. The little girl must have come to the party early. She was enjoying the setting and sounds of a tea party for grown-ups. My friend was deeply touched.

We have met our first youthful ghost here at the Pink House Café. Spirit children are not uncommon in Independence. They are playful and attached to their places. We will be meeting more youngsters.

CHAPTER 18

INDEPENDENCE/POLK COUNTY WOMAN'S CLUB AND THE HISTORIC INDEPENDENCE LIBRARY

O ur next stop is another building moved to its current site. But where the prior building was moved with modern methods, this one was not. This is the Independence/Polk County Woman's Club. I had always called it the "women's club" until I was corrected by a good friend and long-time member: "It's a woman's club," she insisted. My friend Betty Lou was sweet and always kind, but when she needed to make a point, she was adamant.

This building, once the First Presbyterian Church, was moved here prior to 1929 via logs, horses and cables or ropes. In this interesting process, the structure is lifted onto rolling logs, cables are attached and horses pull the cables through a windlass. Though the horses are moving in a circular direction, the structure is moved straight toward its destination. It is a slow process. When a log under the trailing edge of the building is exposed, it is moved by hand to take its place at the leading edge. This process is repeated until the structure at its new site, and all logs are removed.

In the case of the Woman's Club, one log was particularly stubborn. It was stuck dead center under the building and would go nowhere. The movers, in exasperation, decided to leave the log where it was. It was a cedar log and would not rot in such a way as to compromise the building. The log stayed, the building settled and now, if you go into the building, kneel down and look across the floor: you will see a gentle center hump above the resting place of the large cedar log.

A fun story was told to me once on Ghost Walk night. A woman was laughing when she exited the building. She said she'd taken ballet lessons

Women's Club and Historic Library. The buildings have been neighbors since 1929. One moved to the site, and the other one was built next to it. *Courtesy the author.*

in that building when she was a girl. Somehow, she'd always felt taller at her lessons than anywhere else—and now she understood why. She must have been placed in the center of her classmates—a budding prima ballerina?—on the highest part of the floor.

HISTORIC INDEPENDENCE LIBRARY

This is one of the more historic corners in town. The historic library is on the southwest corner, built in 1929. Across the street is a church building that is more than 130 years old.

Today the historic library is home to the Monmouth-Independence Chamber of Commerce and Visitor Center, the Independence Downtown Association and the Friends of the Independence Public Library. You might think it is crowded in here, but everyone lives and works in harmony. However, there is one rule that we must all follow: never, never go to the basement.

You see, this historic building is haunted in its own way by several animal species. There are frogs in the basement, and Vaux's Swifts come down its chimney and nest in the cellar. Starlings come through any available opening to camp between the walls. Who knows what else lurks there?

There is a little more to the story now. In 2012, the basement was shored up and resealed. It means that one recent incident from the previous year probably won't happen again.

The chamber manager was working in the back and heard meowing. It sounded close. She looked out the windows and checked with staff in the front to see if anyone heard it. Nobody else had. Back to work she went, thinking it must have been a strange sound effect caused by the unusual configuration of the back office.

The meowing began again. It sounded so close. Her gaze swept the basement door and dismissed it as a source—after all, the basement was closed up completely, except for the chimney access, barely big enough for a tiny bird to navigate.

The meowing continued, and finally, as a last resort, she opened the basement door.

Out strolled a large and healthy-looking yellow cat. The cat was friendly but in no way desperate for food or attention. The cat visited all the staff members, accepted attention, disdained food and then began standing at the low windows, looking out with longing. The manager asked if it would like to go out, walked it to the back door in another part of the building and the kitty exited, never to be seen again.

Remember the friend who had made sure the neighboring building was identified as the "woman's" club? This dear friend and dedicated community volunteer had passed on earlier in the year. The chamber manager admits that, upon seeing the cat, she thought it was entirely possible that Betty Lou had come back for a visit. It would have been just like her to go to a classic building that attracted readers and volunteers.

CHAPTER 19

HOMES ALONG THE WAY

Many homes in our town have ghostly stories associated with them. We don't visit them on the Ghost Walk. For the sake of privacy, neither do we disclose owners' names or addresses. But the stories about these homes, when told in anonymity, are fair game! In fact, some pretty chilling tales have been told to us about houses along or near the Ghost Walk route. Though the Ghost Walk visits businesses and public buildings, on the longer stretches of the walk, we do group shares of stories attached to local homes.

In one home on South Main Street, there is a small, windowless, concrete-walled room under the basement stairs. Inside the room are some red splotches that have resisted all attempts at removal. Owners, in a moment of curiosity, had the red substance tested, and it was found to be blood. On the underside of the stair railing are words crudely carved into the wood: "Help Me."

Also on Main Street, another home from the early 1900s has a resident ghost upstairs. Families occupying the home from the beginning have known and accepted the ghost. The spirit is benevolent, sometimes a little mischievous. Opening doors, moving small objects, cold spots and soft whispers are its reported activities. Curiously, this is a location where women are more likely to sense a spirit. Men generally have nothing of note to say about this house.

A couple blocks away, a genteel, two-story white home has a noteworthy history. Today, when soldiers return from battle, they may be afflicted

This house is often for sale. *Courtesy the author.*

with post-traumatic stress disorder (PTSD). Though the term is new, PTSD is not a new disorder. The term that earlier generations used was "shellshocked."

At the end of World War I, shellshocked troops were coming home in droves. They needed assistance and returned to a nation unprepared to deliver it. Sanitariums and asylums were the care facilities of the day. Asylums were often homes of those involuntarily committed, while sanitariums were places people could check into for a much-needed rest. There was no stigma attached to checking into a sanitarium, and it was often considered the privilege of the wealthy.

Now, however, many, many soldiers needed immediate care. Long-term domestic patients were turned out into temporary quarters while the established places cared for the servicemen. To handle the overflow, many private homes were pressed into service as makeshift sanitariums. One of the homes in Independence was used for this purpose.

The home may have been a temporary asylum, but there were some long-term residual effects. Homeowners tell us that they still experience moved or lost items. Hair is frequently pulled, and cold spots are often felt. Some of the patients apparently left their mark behind. Or maybe they liked the new quarters so well—a nice home instead of a dreary institution—that they decided on a long-term stay.

On our route, we will pass a home that is often for sale. Sometimes it has been for sale for several years, and it has been sold and then put quickly back on the market again. Its condition is not related to the economy; it is related to ghostly activity. Buyers have come and gone when the activity gets to be too much for them. Potential buyers come to look and then back away. Renters cannot even be found. One of the paranormal groups is eyeing this house as a potential headquarters, if they can afford the rent.

Finally, there is a home along these back streets that has a one-trick spirit. This story was told to me by a vendor at our Fourth of July celebration. She recalled visiting her grandmother in Independence and the ghost that shared space with Grandma. Grandma had nicknamed her spectral resident Jeffrey. Jeffrey was known for one odd ability: he could levitate the VCR. The vendor told me she and her cousins would run into the living room and call out for Grandma when they saw the VCR floating above the TV. Grandma would come in and say, "Jeffrey, put that down!" Down went the VCR. This was a constant for visits for many years. No recent information about VCR levitation has surfaced, so perhaps Jeffrey's talent didn't extend to newer technology.

The stories that have been collected about some of the homes fit the essence of Independence spirits—sometimes whimsical or impish, often mysterious, but not malevolent.

Many of the stories of area homes are shared at this point in the Ghost Walk because there is a long trek of two blocks between the last stop at the library and the next one at the Heritage Museum. The ghostly action picks up markedly as we progress on this walk. The museum is a hot spot indeed.

CHAPTER **20**

THE HERITAGE MUSEUM

In 1888, what is now the Heritage Museum was built to be the First Baptist Church of Independence. The Heritage Museum holds artifacts and written history for Independence and the surrounding communities, from 1840 to present. The museum is part of the National Historic District that includes all of downtown Independence. In 1888, you could build an elaborate church for just $4,000.

There are several strange tales associated with it, though oddly enough, none are in conjunction with the building's near-century as a church. The ghostly history of the museum did not begin until it was abandoned as a church and reopened as a museum.

A local writer had an office in the museum for a while. Clearly, he had chosen it as a site for quiet reflection and uninterrupted writing. But it didn't work out that way for him.

He had not been working there long when he heard a meeting going on. Surprised because the museum wasn't open that day, he followed the sounds to a closed door. Little was beyond the door, but a meeting was in progress nonetheless. He listened to the subdued voices and gathered that some kind of church meeting was going on. A church meeting would not have been out of place, since the building had been a church for almost one hundred years. Some more attention to the sounds and he determined that what he was hearing was a blackball vote being carried out. The sounds ended. Meeting over?

He also heard and saw other things in the museum that convinced him it was not an ideal workspace. When he left, it was with a vow to never return.

Heritage Museum. *Courtesy the author.*

Blackball kit at the Independence Masonic Lodge. *Courtesy the author.*

To explain further about this particular incident, a blackball vote is an old meeting tool used to rid a group of an offending member. A large supply of black and white balls is provided for voters. Each voter audibly casts a single ball into the ballot box under cover of the box or of a combination of a cloth and the box itself, so that observers can see who votes but not how he or she is voting. When all voting is complete, the box is opened and the balls displayed: all present can immediately see the result, without any means of knowing which members are objecting. Just one black ball among the white was enough to oust a potential member or kill an issue.

There is in fact a blackball ballot box in the Masonic lodge, and it is still used in extreme situations. The door on the top opens to reveal a fist-sized hole so the voter can slip his whole hand into the box and release his vote secretly.

Returning to the museum, there is a picture that, when photographed, may carry on it a second scene superimposed on the glass. It is a sort of ghostly portrait on a solid portrait. This first was noticed when some schoolchildren were taking pictures on a class field trip. The phenomenon has happened several times since but with no predictability.

The museum is an old structure and is full of warrens and small rooms. The director says that in the process of opening up, there are twenty-seven light switches, strings and chains that must be flipped and pulled. There are many doors that will open or close of their own accord. The museum has a basement, and that is where research is often done and where undisplayed artifacts are stored. One room has been filled with mannequins, and more

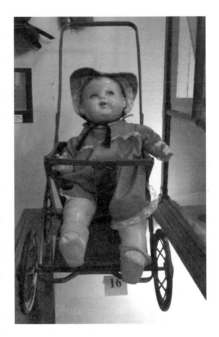

Doll and carriage displayed at the Heritage Museum. *Courtesy the author.*

than one person swears to movement among them. The basement is a more demonstrative area for who or whatever else inhabits the museum. Displeasure or disagreement is expressed through slamming or unexpectedly locked doors. The museum director has developed a regular practice of discussing plans out loud with the invisible residents, preparing them for changes about which they could have an opinion.

The most recent oddity is a moving doll. When I learned about the doll, I went to see it. I expected to find a small porcelain doll that could have shifted or fallen, causing the appearance of movement. What I saw and subsequently learned was quite a surprise. This is no small doll. It is at least twenty-four inches in length and sits upright in an old-fashioned stroller. Doll and stroller both move, and not mere inches, but from display to display, floor to shelf and room to room, all on their own.

CHAPTER 21

150 C STREET AND OTHER SIDE-STREET LOCALES

The building at 150 C Street was built in 1913. Early tenants were Ed Owen's and Dick Gaines's Pool & Cigar Store. A pool and cigar store would have been perfect for C Street, which was once the main street in Independence and for years was lined with bars and taverns. Pool playing and cigar smoking would have been natural pastimes for this same clientele. Despite its surroundings, this building was one of the few places on C Street that was not a tavern at least once in its life. At one time, there was surely signage on the front, as well as a mural on the side of the building, so advertisement could be aimed in two directions. Today there are remnants of a mural on the east side of the building. It remains the only testament on the street to its party-town past.

Later it was occupied by Foster's Plumbing through the 1950s. A dry cleaner took up residence for three decades. Now the space is operated by the second generation of this same family, and they have upgraded it to be a lovely scrapbooking store.

Before the scrapbook store opened, some mischief happened. The owner had glass shelves installed on the walls, and they were filled with patterns and displays. She was very surprised to discover that, on the morning before her grand opening, the glass shelves had somehow moved laterally, as if going to the left and down. They lay unbroken on the floor, but their contents were scattered haphazardly beneath and beyond where they had been shelved.

This building has had some very human haunting, as well. People, from time to time, have secretly taken up residence in the second story. Recently

Mural on corner of 150 C Street. *Courtesy of the author.*

the police had to assist with an eviction of a second-story dweller and his many marijuana plants.

There are a couple one-block stretches on the Ghost Walk route that are long and dark. Walking is done with caution because the sidewalks are dicey in places. This is particularly true on B Street, where a humongous tulip tree appears to grow up and out of the sidewalk. It's one of the largest tulip trees I've ever seen and once earned the jaw-dropping awe and respect of a visiting arborist. This passage, especially, we take with care. And the setting is perfect for intimate stories told by host and guests alike.

One year, my group was coming down this dark area, and someone was saying we should have actors to make it more fun and to add surprises. Then someone pointed out that there was a police car down at the park, a block and a half ahead of us. Another voice added, "It's probably there on purpose, for effect!"

Suddenly, from one of the backyards, a large and imposing man jumped out onto the sidewalk. "Aarrgghh!" he yelled. "I just beat the s**t out of a guy down in the park, and I'm going to do it to you too if you don't get out of my way!" He was waving his arms, looking menacing and definitely angry.

Knowing this wasn't part of the walk, I had been herding my folks toward the opposite side of the street. When the man finished his diatribe, he started off, loping away from the park and the police. As he left, my group applauded the "actor" and shared their praise for a trick well played. I told them repeatedly that it was not a planned or staged event. "Sure," "Right," "Good job," they all said.

Less than three minutes later, as we were sharing another story, a policeman came up to our group. He got everyone's attention and then asked if we had seen an angry, upset and possibly confused guy anywhere around our position. "Yes, yes," everyone replied, some with a little laughter. The policeman reported, "He was just involved in a criminal assault in the park." Stunned silence. "Did you see where he went?"

The group, almost as a unit, turned and pointed in the direction the hollering man had gone. The policeman thanked them and continued his pursuit. The man was quickly caught, in part because my group gave such specific direction.

Ghost Walk groups bond quickly. It doesn't take long for "the" host to become "our" host. "Our" group shortly becomes "the best" group. Hosts encourage this bonding because the experience guests have is so much better because of it.

Before the incident of the yelling man, my group had securely bonded. The incident on the dark walk only served to deepen that bond. I am sure that many of them are still pleased that they helped catch the bad guy on the night of the Ghost Walk.

CHAPTER 22

SPERLING BUILDING

Two of the most haunted blocks in Independence begin here, at 114 South Main, the Sperling Building. Today there is a restaurant on the corner and a bar waiting for a new landlord.

This anchor building on the northwest corner was the project of an important early resident of Independence. Albert Sperling built the Sperling Hotel in 1913, after a fire had demolished the Little Palace Hotel a block away. Local historical information says that it was originally named the Lerona Hotel after Sperling's two daughters, Leona and Rowena. When it opened, the building had a bank, dining room, bakery and sample room on the first floor, with the hotel occupying the second floor. It also boasted steam heat, a new and fancy feature.

This building has suffered a long identity crisis. Name confusion has plagued this location from the beginning. Some of it has spooky origins. The Sperling Building was recently the site of Lenora's Ghost, a popular tavern. "The Ghost," as it was familiarly known, is the center of a lot of haunted activity. In fact, the tavern was named for a ghost. But was her name Lenora? We just aren't sure.

Lerona was a name given to the location by the building's owner. That name was a creation coming from the combination of his two daughters' names. In the last days of World War I, when the building was still known as the Lerona Hotel, a young woman was lodging in the hotel upstairs. We do not know her name, but because this incident occurred in the Lerona Hotel, the woman's name became Lerona in the retelling of the tale.

114 South Main Street under construction. *Courtesy Heritage Museum.*

The fine hotel was a destination for many important dignitaries. *Courtesy Heritage Museum.*

Lerona was an orphan. Her parents, hop farmers, both died from tuberculosis when she was sixteen. There was a great deal of debt on the farm, and she went to work to pay it off.

She met a young man who had enlisted in the army because he was inspired to fight for his country. World War 1 was raging in Europe. Lerona and the soldier fell in love and were married just days before he shipped out. She would have left with him, but she still had debt on the farm to repay and was forced to remain behind to work.

Time passed, and Lenora heard the good news that the end of the war would be coming soon. Even better, her new husband was being sent home. But on his way from the battlefield to his point of departure, he was shot and killed by one of the last shots fired in the war.

Poor Lerona. While working at the tavern and waiting for the return of her sweetheart, she received the sad news via telegram. She was distraught. Her last act was to throw herself through a stained-glass transom window, dropping from the top of a very tall two-story structure to the floor of the hotel. She died on impact, and her blood, it is said, permanently stained the wood flooring. Repeated scrubbings always fail to remove the discoloration.

According to the Pacific Paranormal Research Society, Lerona was a little more experienced than just a poor farming girl. She was, according to their information, manager of the hotel, a full bar and a profitable brothel. This story tells us that Lerona and her soldier weren't married yet; he was still her fiancé. He had been stationed at Camp Adair, fifteen miles south of Independence, and from there he was deployed to the front lines. Shortly before the war ended, Lerona received the news that her fiancé had been killed in battle. She decided to join him. She climbed the steps onto the roof of her building and plunged headfirst through the stained-glass skylight. Her body crashed through to the hardwood floor in front of the bar.

Now the name confusion comes into play. After being a hotel and several other eating/drinking establishments, the ground floor of the corner building was divided into two parts. The north half became a restaurant and stayed that way. Well, most of the time…there was that six-month period when pornographic movies were made in the space, and all the windows were papered over.

The south half of the building became a bar and has stayed that way since. The bar's manager was aware of some other presence in the building. During a remodel, the bar decided to pay homage to the ghost.

Paperwork was drawn up and taken to the county seat. Lerona's Ghost was the name chosen to honor the girl/woman who met her end through a skylight window. But at the county, a spelling error occurred. The *R* and the *N* in Lerona were switched, and it became Lenora's Ghost. The error wasn't noticed until later. Rather than go through the clerical effort to sort out the name confusion, owners simply called the place Lenora's.

Conversations with the manager of Lenora's Ghost yielded this information: the ghost is a troublemaker. "Mostly she just moves stuff around," he said, "but we always feel like she's around." He knew about the supposed haunting when he took the job but wanted to see for himself what it was all about. His attitude is slightly changed now. "It kinda puts you in a hurry to get out if you're here all alone," he said.

"You can still see the original bloodstain where she fell through," said the manager. Indeed, anyone interested in seeing the spot where Lenora died can visit the bar and see for himself or herself.

It seems like since she was not able to leave with the man she loved, she chose to never leave at all. Strange occurrences still take place, reminding visitors of her presence. "She's not a mean ghost; she's more mischievous," the manager said. "When she visits, she moves things. Chairs fall, and one time a cooler door flew open and scared the crap out of me."

Skeptics may claim those were just coincidences, but the manager feels otherwise. "I totally believe. I've had ghost chasers come in, and they took 750 infrared pictures," he said. "They were looking for blurs, and in two pictures they actually found orbs. We have definite scientific proof of paranormal activity."

Many strange sounds, voices and footsteps have been heard in the vacant upper stories of the building. Dogs, when brought in, react keenly to the upper reaches of the building, howling and whining.

There have been many, many sightings of the forlorn woman that is said to haunt Lenora's. Sometimes she is seen inside, as mentioned in one of the stories. Other times she's seen crossing Main Street but never reaching the other side. Is she trying to leave or just needing a change of scenery?

Recently we heard from a woman who, when outside Lenora's, looked in through the window and saw woman walking down the stairs. Later, when she turned to look in again, there was no woman—and no stairs.

The latest story I heard concerned a woman headed to teach an evening Jazzercise class. She was in her car, driving south on Main Street, two blocks from her destination. There, in front of Lenora's Ghost and just stepping into the street from the sidewalk, was a woman dressed completely in white. She appeared to be in a long, old-fashioned dress.

The instructor slowed to a stop and watched the woman pass very close by the front of her car. The woman's clothing was a bright white, clearly visible under the streetlights. But her head was veiled or shrouded in some sort of covering, her face averted as she walked.

As the woman in white touched the sidewalk, the instructor moved forward, checking her rearview mirror. First check, there she was, the woman in white, just getting fully onto the sidewalk. Intrigued, the instructor made a quick double-check, and the woman was gone. There was no white clothing visible, which should have been easy to spot. The sidewalk on the corner was well lit; she should have been clearly visible. But there was nothing. The woman in white was gone.

At the Jazzercise class, the instructor related her story with excitement. Speculation on the woman's identity soon surfaced. It was Lenora/Lerona, possibly veiled in wedding clothing. Several classmates confirmed that Lenora/Lerona was frequently seen but said that she always disappeared when reaching the sidewalk after she crossed the street.

The instructor was perplexed. She had seen everything so clearly as the mysterious woman passed in front of her car. She even recalled some of the patterning in the dress. Yes, she thought, it could have been a wedding dress. The veiled face fit that explanation too. But where did she go?

There is one newer story that, while not ghostly, confirms the name confusion surrounding this building. We know the hotel was originally the Lerona. We know it is now called Lenora's because of a typo at the county office. When doing some remodeling and cleaning, a tile entryway piece was discovered. Nobody knew how long it had been buried under dirt and grime. The tiles spelled out "LERONA." The man who was doing the cleaning was taken aback. He told his co-worker that Lerona was his mother's name.

Names! There's Leona, Rowena, Lerona and Lenora all attached to the building. But no firm name connections to the actual ghost exist. Poor woman: no fiancé, no husband, no name. And yet, she stays.

To wrap up the saga of Lenora/Lerona, here's one last story. Several years back, a Ghost Walk took a particularly naughty turn. My group and I were out in front listening to Vidal Pena, manager of Lenora's Ghost, who was quoted earlier. He was telling us all about the ghost's playfulness, from brushing up against customers to pulling barmaids' hair.

The LERONA Hotel's name captured in long-hidden tile. *Courtesy the author.*

The woman standing next to me asked, "Is that what I think it is?" I turned to look and began to laugh. "Yes, I believe it is," I replied.

Inside, a party was going on. A young woman was having a birthday party with her friends. As a gift, her friends had hired a male stripper.

To the credit of the establishment, the party was toward the back. And it was in a closed off area with a half-wall. But the girls were laughing noisily, and there were special lights. It was attention grabbing.

By this time, many of the female heads on the Ghost Walk had turned to enjoy the show inside of the bar. Meanwhile, our site host was calling for everyone's attention, saying that the show was up in front, and he had more stories to tell.

Several women shook their heads and laughed, but they did turn to the front.

The most engaging aspect of the party inside was that the half wall was very short, and the young male dancer was very tall.

A new story has been added to the Lenora's saga with what is now known as the "Chippendale's Ghost Walk."

CHAPTER 23

MAIN STREET ANTIQUES, 144 SOUTH MAIN STREET

This building was erected in 1880. The original owners of the structure, Mr. Belt and Mr. Whitaker, operated a furniture business for ten years. There are still remnants of signage that says "Whitaker Furniture." Extensive remodeling and upgrades have been done to the Main Street Antiques building. As mentioned, it began as a furniture store and became a Chinese restaurant in 1900. The building housed various businesses up until the present. At this writing, it is now a well-respected antique store.

Today, Main Street Antiques is a jewel on Main Street. This is the building that led the downtown renaissance. Main Street Antiques is a two-story building with residential space above and commercial beneath. There is a beautiful staircase that sweeps to the upstairs in grandeur. The owner has made his upstairs residence a showplace, too, with a lovely back balcony cascaded with trailing plants. Even the tiny alley between the Sperling Building and Main Street Antiques has unique charm.

Main Street Antiques is also the source of a traveling ghost. Main Street Antiques has a little boy in residence. He has been seen often, and he is never without his favorite plaything: a red bouncy ball. His original and, we presume, continuing main residence is at Main Street Antiques.

Imagine the fun a little boy could have in a store full of antiques. Just think what fun it would be to run up and down the beautiful staircase and what a good place that would be to bounce a ball. Sounds and evidence of all this, and more, were happening regularly in Main Street Antiques. The more the little boy played and bounced his ball through the store and up the stairs,

144 South Main Street. *Courtesy City of Independence.*

the more brazen he became. Finally, all this activity became an unbearable nuisance—and sleep killer—for the owner, Dan. At his wit's end, he stood at the top of the stairs one day and announced loudly that a deal would have to be struck. The little boy could have the downstairs at night and the upstairs during the day. The owner needed to have some separation, some peace and some sleep.

It appeared that the deal worked, because nightly interruptions were fewer and contained in the downstairs area. There may have been sounds from above in the day, but the former noticeable mischief in the store during business hours tapered off to nearly nothing. Dan was relieved and says the deal has stuck.

But an interesting thing happened. Was it because of the agreement? The little boy and his ball have been seen in other buildings. Did his agreement with Dan release him to travel? He has been spotted several times in the building due south of Main Street Antiques and in another building a block farther south. Or was he released because of the extensive remodeling on Main Street?

As remodeling and upgrading spread from Main Street Antiques outward, so did the visibility of the little boy. Did all the carpentry and renovation open doorways? Or did it stir up a past that welcomed the little boy? We don't know.

CHAPTER 24

RAGIN' RIVER STEAK COMPANY

Built around 1880, this building first served as a grocery store until, in 1888, it became a furniture store, which it would remain for nearly seven decades. It changed hands several times but continued to sell furniture. One of our local elders, Al Oppliger, has a clear memory of most of the businesses on Main Street, including this one. In fact, he probably even worked there as a youth. In 1976, the building became AMVETS Post 1776.

In the days when this building housed the AMVETS, there was a lot of activity that was rarely mentioned. AMVETS maintained a very active bar, and it was often under the scrutiny of the police. Likely the patrons had other things on their mind besides sighting spirits. We were mainly unaware of this activity until there was opportunity for a casual conversation with a recent post commander of the Amvets. In one of my downtown walk-arounds, I met with him and happened to mention the Ghost Walk and said that downtown seemed a pretty spectrally busy place.

"No question of that!" he replied. Then he recounted several incidences when he had seen and felt things in the building. Several times, he said, he thought he'd seen someone out of the corner of his eye. He knew it to be a human form, but when he looked straight on, there was nothing there. He also remembered often walking through unexplained cold spots and coming away with distinct shivers. The AMVETS had recently opened a courtyard in the back of the building. Activity flowed into the newly extended space. The post commander said sightings and cold spots occurred outside, too.

When Ragin' River Steak Company took over the space, a full-scale remodel was begun. Several new stories come from the time of that remodeling. Here is one of the best:

154 South Main Street, today's Ragin' River, 1910. *Courtesy City of Independence.*

154 Main Street, 1935. *Courtesy Heritage Museum.*

It was the night before the electrical inspector was to come and approve all the work in the restaurant, but there was still work to be done around the mezzanine. The grand opening was less than two weeks away. The restaurant owner contacted his electrician, a good friend. The owner and the electrician made an agreement that the final electrical work would be done at night so it would be completed by the time the inspector was due to arrive at 9:00 a.m. The agreement included that the owner would leave the back door unlocked and have a dozen or so ladders propped up against the mezzanine edge so the electrician's crew could move quickly.

The owner finished his work and locked the front. Then he went to the back and left an outside light on and the door unlocked. He got in his car to go home. But something nagged at him…did he leave the door unlocked as promised? Back to the restaurant he went to check. To his dismay, the back light was off, and the door was locked. He unlocked and turned the light on and left again. Still, he had a worried feeling. He drove around the block and peeked up the alley behind the building. No lights! Back to the restaurant he went, to once again find the door locked and the lights off. For a third time, he unlocked the door and put the lights on. One more look on the way confirmed the lights were still on, so he left. He expected his electrician friend would call if there were further problems.

A couple of hours later, the owner received a call. It was indeed from his friend the electrician. "Are you trying to mess with me?" as the electrician. "Was the door locked?" the owner queried. "No, the door was open, and the lights were on, just like you said. It's something else." The owner was puzzled. Then his friend said, "You've got to come here to see this."

The owner took another trip back to the restaurant, where he was met by his friend. "I thought you were going to set all the ladders for us," he said. "I did," said the owner. "Well, come and look." His friend led him inside.

In the middle of the large restaurant space, there were ladders. They were not propped up against the mezzanine, as the owner had left them. Instead, all dozen or so ladders were laid in a crosshatched tower in the middle of the room. Nobody was able to explain it, then or now.

Other stories related about the building sound like some we've already heard: body-less footsteps, opening doors with nobody there, cold spots and mischievous acts. But these stories took on a new flavor one day. The owner was chatting with the proprietor of Main Street Antiques about the strange things happening at the new restaurant. The owner went into detail about things being moved around, lights turning on and off and doors being locked and unlocked until the antique dealer stopped him, saying, "So, have you seen the little boy?"

The restaurant owner didn't know what to say. Little boy? What little boy?

The men finished their conversation, and the owner headed back to the restaurant. Not many days afterward, he saw a red ball come bouncing into the restaurant and back to the kitchen. Seeing no one who might have tossed the ball into the building, he tossed it back out again.

Did the little boy find entry into the restaurant by sending his ball in first, a spectral envoy? Possibly, because from then on, sightings of the little boy inside the restaurant became more frequent.

One of the people in the crew was very, very frightened of ghosts. The little boy, however, must have found him a lovely playmate. In the building there is an electronics room that is narrow and deep. When this room is open and the light is on, a weird square of light projects into the dark restaurant. One evening, the little boy played hide-and-seek with the leery worker. The boy would hunker down on the floor, peek his head out so that it was framed by the square of light and wait until the worker saw him. Then, pop, back he went into the room and out of sight. After two more of the here—not here appearances from the boy, the worker yelled for the owner, thinking him the perpetrator. There was no answer, so the worker went to check the room. Nothing there. The game ended, and the next morning, the worker chided the owner for playing tricks on him. "Impossible," said the owner. "It wasn't me. I was in Eugene last night."

The ball bouncing in and out of the restaurant is not uncommon. In fact, the owner has occasionally told a full house of guests not to be surprised to see something red come whizzing into the restaurant. Not to worry, he'll take care of it. The ball has been seen coming back into the street, and when someone goes to retrieve it, it has already been taken away.

The restaurant is now under new ownership. The new owner continues to have interactions with the little boy. The boy's new game is to put his fingerprints in dusty spots. Why does the new owner think the little boy is responsible for the fingerprints? Because they are in the dust on the top of one of the black fabric air return vents that are suspended a foot from the ceiling in the restaurant. It wouldn't be a problem leaving them there, except that in one space the vent crosses into clear public view and is well lit, and tiny fingerprints are clearly visible. Someone must climb up to dust regularly. The last time I was at the restaurant, I spotted a brand-new set of fingerprints, fresh from the last dusting.

CHAPTER 25
MAXINE'S

The Heritage Museum describes the building housing Maxine's by saying, "Downstairs, the building served as a general merchandise store and later a dry goods store until 1940. The upper floor was used by the International Order of the Odd Fellows Fraternal Order from 1902 through the mid 1970's. Legend says building being was once a speakeasy and/or brothel, and the presence of a door with a peephole would lend credence to this."

According to the website for Maxine's Ballroom:

> *The building that now houses Maxine's Ballroom was built in 1884 as a Masonic Hall, but sold within a few years to the Odd Fellows, in whose hands it remained until the 1950s.*
>
> *The Odd Fellows used the top floor, which included a large and small ballroom, kitchen and a warren of small offices and passageways (complete with secret password speaking tubes and sliding peepholes), for lodge meetings and dances. During the war years, the ballrooms were opened to the public on many occasions, and USO dances were regularly held upstairs for the entertainment of soldiers stationed at Camp Adair.*
>
> *Once the Independence Odd Fellows disbanded, the upstairs rooms gradually fell into disrepair, until Maxine's 2011 restoration to 1880s ballroom splendor.*

In a continuing remodel of the upper floor, it was also discovered that the building had been a boxing club. This was once a popular pastime for local

World War II parade, circa 1945, at the corner of Main and C Streets looking to the west. This was the functional main thoroughfare in the early days, as the ferry dropped people and wagons off at the base of C Street. Ash Creek Clinic, 194 South Main, is on the right, sporting an overhang and upper facing no longer in existence. *City of Independence.*

gents. There are stories about local champions, but they are sketchy at best and describe amateur activities. Was there betting? Probably. In the remodel, wallpaper was peeled back to reveal artwork promoting the club. The style would date to perhaps the 1940s or 1950s. It appears that the front half of the long second story was used for the Odd Fellows hall and the back for the Boxing Club. The Odd Fellows and their stated mission are of importance to the story that comes to us from the second story of the building.

Odd Fellows organizations are not as prevalent today as they were one hundred years ago. Each lodge was independently founded, and each seemed to craft its individual mission. Terms were similar, however: "…to visit the sick, relieve the distressed, bury the dead and educate the orphan," "…favor no person for their wealth, frown on none for their poverty" and other similar credos.

I have been told that a determined mission of the Independence Odd Fellows was to make sure that every man was given a proper burial. It was unforgivable to them to allow a man to rest in eternity in the potter's field, unremarked by his peers. This particular Odd Fellows organization had extensive ritual and ceremony that spoke to their mission. One of the artifacts they used was a coffin. The complete artifact would have had a skeleton inside the coffin to bring the ceremony into full accord with its symbolism. In fraternal symbolism—Odd Fellow, Masons and similar organizations—the meeting rituals often demonstrate or exemplify the mission of the group as a whole. I've been around Masonry for a while and have seen ritual meant to portray their mission. I see this happening at the Odd Fellows lodge in Independence in much the same way.

Local stories tell us that a gentleman by the name of Max was a devoted Odd Fellow. The Odd Fellows did indeed have a coffin, but Max knew it to be empty, so the ceremony was not as rich as it could be. Being the ardent member he was, he announced to his brothers that he was changing his will. When the time came where he passed from this earth, his wishes were that his brothers accept his body and have it prepared to become the official skeleton-artifact of the fraternity. He willed himself to be the skeleton in the coffin.

The stories go on to say that Max did pass away, and it happened during an Odd Fellows meeting, further proving his devotion. After family matters were completed, the group had Max's body prepared. Max's skeleton was placed in the coffin in the Odd Fellows hall. The ceremonies would now be complete and even more meaningful.

The membership of the lodge declined, and the Odd Fellows fraternity in Independence disbanded. New owners took over the building. They first remodeled the downstairs, and it became Ash Creek Animal Clinic. After a few more years, the owners turned their interest to the upstairs space and began exploring. Picture their surprise when, in their investigation of the upper floor, they found a coffin—and within it, a skeleton!

It must have been a novel discovery, and they must have mused for quite a while about what to do with their newfound treasure. At some point, the discovery was made among papers and other coffin contents that the skeletal remains belonged to an Odd Fellow named Max. In deference to his identification, the owners began to call him by name. They also observed that, at some point, Max had been wired together and colored, as if for use as an anatomical teaching tool. We don't know if this was standard procedure for skeletons in Odd Fellow ceremonies. Nor do we know if this was part of Max's plan to make himself as useful in the afterlife as possible.

194 South Main is located on one of the most busy corners in old Independence history. *Courtesy Heritage Museum.*

Maxine's, second story of 194 South Main. *Courtesy Dr. Robert Archer.*

At last, the owners made the determination that they didn't want to keep the coffin or its contents. In a seemingly natural move, they contacted the proprietor of Main Street Antiques to see if he was interested.

Certainly, he would accept Max and his coffin. Max had wonderful provenance. In fact, Dan decided, he would make a delightful window display. So Max took his place, front and center, tilted at an appealing angle, in the main window of Main Street Antiques.

Not long after, many shoppers were strolling down Main Street and stopping to look at Max in the window. One of these lookers was an off-duty Oregon State policeman. He was perplexed by Max and decided to find out more.

In the shop, he spoke with Dan about his window display, and Dan told him what he knew. The policeman then asked the owner, "Do you know, sir, that it is illegal to traffic in human remains?" Well, the owner hadn't seen it that way before, but when the information was delivered by the police, it changed his perspective. He offered the skeleton and coffin to the policeman on the spot.

From here the story gets a little fragmented, but the salient points remain. We presume it must have been a slow time for the state police forensics lab, because Max ended up on one of the tables in that facility. His skeleton was analyzed, perhaps for teaching purposes. That might have made Max proud.

But it ended up that Max had no say in the matter after all. The skeleton was determined to be that of a female, and a Native American female, at that. In the interest of doing the right thing, the state police repatriated not-Max to a local tribe.

Meanwhile, remodeling in the space above Ash Creek Clinic was continuing. Owners had made plans to begin with a meeting space and then progress to a dance hall that could be used for instruction and for social occasions.

When the whole story found its way back to the owners, they took one finishing step that wraps up the story quite nicely.

In honor of Max not being Max after all, the new space and eventual dance hall was declared to be "Maxine's."

CHAPTER 26
COOPER BUILDING

Built in 1889, the Cooper Building has a checkered past. J.S. Cooper originally built a one-story saloon on the corner of Main and C Streets. That building was taken down and replaced three years later by a three-story building called the J.S. Cooper Block Building. It has housed, in its lifetime, a saloon, doctor and dentist offices, probably a brothel, a popular gambling house and a steakhouse. It currently awaits its next (living) owner. Long-standing reports say that footsteps, strange voices, laughter and even screams have been heard in the unoccupied upper stories of the building.

That is the history of the building, including some spectral additions. Now let's delve into the modern happenings here, as they are many. This building has a reputedly high incidence of suicides. In fact, it is believed to be the building with the highest rate of suicide in town. Owners of this building have been known to take their own lives with alarming regularity. The prior owner stood in the bar area and shot himself in the head. The bullet passed through his head and traveled farther to leave a noticeable chip in the large leaded and beveled mirror that hangs over the bar. This tragedy, which happened just twenty years ago, was the last—or latest—in a string of suicides.

We do not really know how to attribute these deaths. Poor business practices? The current owner has left the building empty for ten years. Sadly, it deteriorates inside and out. The destruction is aided by the fact that there is an open well in the basement of this building. It encourages mold and mildew growth. There is record of a well being dug but no reason why it was installed.

Cooper Building. *Courtesy the author.*

The mannequins on the second story have their own ghostly history. One morning, one of the mannequins, which occupied a spot well back from the sill, was found lying on the street. The second-story window was broken. Did the mannequin "jump" to its death? That was hard to believe. When I told the story of the mannequins, this is where it ended, until one Ghost Walk night. A woman who was with another group came running over. She had heard me finish the story and was saying, "No, there's more." I asked her to share details with my group.

"I was here when it happened," she said, "standing right over there on the corner." She pointed to the opposite corner from where my group

Cooper Building, corner of Main and C Streets. *Courtesy the author.*

stood. "I saw movement upstairs, and suddenly the mannequin was right at the window. It pitched forward, through the glass, and fell to the sidewalk. I looked and looked. There was nobody up there to push it."

Apparently the dummy was despondent and decided to end it all.

In the building, the second floor is divided into smaller offices. They ring the steepled area and are identified by the windows that are mid-way up. This is another location where tape recorders have caught yells, screams of "Fire, Fire!" and other bits and pieces of phrases and words. According to history, these offices were occupied by doctors and dentists. It would not have been unusual for yelling and screaming to emanate from these offices, especially in days before proper anesthetic.

In these upper windows, figures have occasionally been spotted watching out over the river. Observers said they assumed they were mannequins, until they walked off. In one particular instance, the person seen at the window was dressed as a dentist from the 1880s or 1890s might have been.

In 2003, a paranormal group visited the building to do a thorough investigation. One of the more spectacular results was a photograph. This photograph was taken with a camera set up with flash, inside, placed in front of a window looking to the dark outside. When the film was developed, there was a picture on the glass and an image of a little girl.

At the top of the steeple there is activity, too. More than once, colored light has been seen pouring out of the windows up top and then bending down toward the street to puddle there. One woman says she saw the phenomenon reflecting in the sky before she got into town and watched it as she drove by the building, checking it in her rearview mirror on her way down Main Street.

When the building was new, there was a grand staircase that came from upstairs to downstairs. It sat toward the rear of the building so that those descending would walk directly into the largest area. The staircase was removed many years ago. When the restaurant was last open, more than one diner reported being seated at a table near where the staircase had been and hearing voices. It sounded to them, without looking, like people coming down a stairway, conversing with each other. When they turned to look, there was, of course, no staircase and no people.

Even the intersection where the Cooper Building stands has activity. An event that seems to be common to many purportedly haunted areas is that of the past superimposing itself on the present. That has happened here, too, when people are close to the Cooper Building. The latest reports have come from drivers who check their rearview mirrors and are surprised to see groups in clothing from the late 1800s strolling on the sidewalks. A view forward reveals the normal scene, but to the rear, it is showing a yesterday long gone.

In its life, the Cooper Building held professional offices on the second floor. The first floor has most often been a restaurant, a bar or both. Live music was a regular feature in this popular watering hole.

A new bit of information recently came to light. In the 1980s, it was said, a gruesome murder occurred behind the Cooper Building. I began some research intended for use in a future Ghost Walk. But my research is still stuck in the early 1900s, when a rather gruesome discovery was made. Perhaps it marked the start of the haunting in this building? Two men of Chinese descent were discovered in a hole in or near the Cooper Building. The hole in which they were found is likely the one currently identified as an open basement well. The Cooper Building is very close to the river. A well would have been redundant, so why is there an open well in the basement? There is no historical explanation to be found. But research of period newspapers taught me that the incident of the "2 Chinamen in the Hole," as headlines described it, made news far outside of Independence. The story of the Cooper Building is clearly very complex.

We have met a little girl at the Pink House Café. A little boy lives at Main Street Antiques and travels outward from there. A little girl was also photographed in the upstairs of the Cooper Building. Several local business owners wondered why there are so many children that figure into local sightings. Speculation takes us in several directions. Were these children victims of floods? Did disease sweep through the town and take young lives? Were they victims of early and less sanitary or knowledgeable medical practices? Or does some of this activity have its roots in a time before our town was even here? We don't know.

Deaths at the Cooper Building are frequent, it seems. They have been talked about for a long time. Besides the two men in the hole, there is the death of the dentist. A dentist in residence there is logical, since the upstairs offices were supposed to be those of doctors and dentists. The dentist stabbed himself. Again, this building is no stranger to suicide.

Another death is that of a gambler. One of the businesses in the Cooper Building was called the Hi-Ho. The Hi-Ho was a very popular local gathering spot. Gambling was a regular sport on site, though probably not a legal one. Believing that a gambler died in the building does not take any stretch of imagination. The difference in the two passings is the spirit that apparently resulted from each. The dentist is said to be kind, but the gambler is pretty mean-spirited. Of the spirits of the two Chinese men, we hear nothing.

There is also reported to be the ghost of a child at the Cooper building, too. At this point, the Pacific Paranormal Society picks up the story.

Number of times investigated: Twice

Ghosts & Historical Value: According to a historian I spoke to at one time, in the mid 1850s before the big flood of 1861, Independence, Oregon was very prosperous as a focal shopping point. It was also said that once the ferry system began running across the Willamette along with the introduction of the railroad in the 1800s that Independence was known to be the town where many of the prominent politicians from Portland and other neighboring cities would frequent. Apparently at the time, "What happens in Independence stays in Independence," and safe from public scrutiny these men could partake in all sorts of debauchery and obtain a get out of jail free card and basically party like a rock star. The J.S. Cooper Block was built up in the late 1890s. In its past it has housed a dentist's office and pharmacy, a speakeasy during prohibition, a restaurant and possible gambling establishment called the HiHo, a lawyer's office, and a restaurant called "Coopers Landing." Probably a brothel (or at least some flapper-attired working girls) are included in there somewhere as noted above.

Known deaths on the property are a dentist with a drinking problem who stabbed himself to death, and a gambler who died downstairs at the card tables.

Ghosts include those listed above as well as the ghost of a little girl (whom the dentist has apparently adopted) and whom we have a photo of, and that of a young girl with short bobbed hair and 1920s attire whom I affectionately call Lila, and which I had the pleasure of capturing on an EVP saying, "Gotta try to talk to her."

Activity Encountered: This place was very interesting and a great place to conduct paranormal research. The frequency of the upstairs area at times can be so unsettling that it can literally make the hair on your arms and the back of your neck stand straight up. It was also extremely difficult to keep any electrical or battery-powered equipment from breaking down. This included everything—our cameras, our recorders, our meters, a $50K news camera and professional sound equipment. Yep, everything. We went through MANY packs of batteries here as well.

One of the more memorable moments was when we were downstairs near the bar. I spoke aloud offering to buy anyone a drink who would like

The apparition of a little girl holding her doll. You can see the white socks on her feet. She is looking down toward the right side. You can see her face if you start at the double reflected lights of the camera flash and look to your right. She is wearing an old-time white dress. *Courtesy Pacific Paranormal Society, photograph by Martina Baker.*

Very good ecto formation. It's always a good night when the TV news crewmen experience inexplicable anomalies during filming on their (expensive) equipment, and you can show them why. *Courtesy Pacific Paranormal Society, photograph by Martina Baker.*

one. The owner's daughter was at the other end of the bar, listening. Up above on the 2nd floor, you could hear heavy footsteps as I (made) the offer. The footsteps above ended directly over the bar area. This type of response was very cool to experience.

We received an astonishing apparition of a little girl reflected in one of the windows as well as a huge formation of ecto looming over [one of the investigators] *while his equipment was acting haywire.*

There has been some noted residual activity at this location as well as the conscious hauntings. This place was and I'm sure still is quite a hotbed of activity, especially EP-wise, and we were not disappointed investigating here. This location taught us a lot about how much ghosts can manipulate frequencies in our environment. Many of the EVSs we recorded were them speaking to each other and amongst themselves. We had never heard them do this before so we were really excited to capture their conversations. A lot of the EVPs we received were scratchy and accompanied by tons of frequency pops. We would love to be able to spend some time in here again some day.

For even more information about the Cooper Building, and to read it in the words of the newsman mentioned above, visit http://www.salem-news.com/articles/october292007/ghost_stories_102607.php.

CHAPTER 27

A LOT IS HAPPENING AT THE
LITTLE MALL ON MAIN

The original building at this location was built in 1888. The second story was added about 1913. Legal maps from the era indicate that the building was occupied by a book and stationary store operated by W.H. and Robert Craven on the first floor. By 1902, the first floor had been divided into a millinery and shoe store. In 1903, Craven became the proprietor of a book and stationery store located in the building. By 1913, Craven had enlarged the building to make room for a soda fountain and candy and cigar counter. The upper story, called Campbell Hall, was used by a fraternal organization as a meeting hall. William Craven served two terms as the mayor of Independence (1908–09) and was elected to the city council. He belonged to the chamber of commerce and held all the chairs at the Independent Order of Odd Fellows. Calbreath's Grocery and Williams' Drug occupied the building in the 1930s. The building functioned as a bowling alley in the 1940s.

The Little Mall on Main is a busy place, spectrally. Several businesses are clustered together in this two-story structure. Many of the people who have worked here have stories to tell. Let's start upstairs.

The front office overlooking the street used to house a beauty salon. The salon owner was subject to with mischievous acts, but also received some interesting bonuses. Whatever entity was active in that part of the building liked to move things around in the presence of customers. Combs and brushes sailed off shelves. Things set down in one place were moved to another. Customers were so familiar with some of the activities that they asked for what amounted to a daily "weather" report when they walked in.

226 South Main Street, circa 1912. *Courtesy Heritage Museum.*

"So, how have things been in here today?" a customer might ask.

"Not too bad," replied the salon manager. "Only some clips and a comb went to the floor."

Another day, the answer would have been, "Pretty wild! One of my ladies was hit by a flying brush. It didn't hurt her, but it sure startled her."

On one memorable afternoon, the shop was full when a loud crash echoed in the small space. "Oh, wow, look at that," said one customer. Everyone turned to see a large metal sculpture lying on the ground. "That's the biggest thing he's ever moved, I think," said another customer. The sculpture, long in place, had "slipped" from the wall.

Most customers had seen enough that the regulars were not especially shocked by the activity. Perhaps the sculpture was dropped so that everyone was reminded there could be more tricks up a spectral sleeve, and they'd better watch out!

The salon owner was pleased, however, with one other regular activity. The entity was generous. Often in the morning she found money lying on the floor or on a counter. Sadly, it was just round money, none of the rectangular green kind. Even so, these little tips were welcome as well as whimsical.

One other very curious thing happened to the salon owner's twin boys. These young boys sometimes came to be at work with their mother. Their mom felt that as long as they stayed in the upstairs area, they were well

226 South Main Street, circa 1950. *Courtesy Heritage Museum.*

confined and safe. She let them play in the stairwell, too. One afternoon, both ran excitedly back into the salon. Between customers, she asked how they were doing. "We've been playing with the little boy," one of the brothers said. "Yeah," said the other. "I can see him, but my brother can't."

The mother was surprised at their finding a playmate and knew right away that he was a friend of a different kind. She said that though her boys were twins, they were different in many ways. One of them regularly saw things his brother did not. But they had full faith in each other and in their differing abilities. Pure childhood play had gone on that day, whether all the players were visible or not.

Next to the space that held the beauty salon is Office K. This windowless space was at one time a conference room. When a larger tenant left, vacating the conference room too, the landlord decided to try to rent the space as a separate facility. Several tenants went in and left in fairly short order. There were unspecific complaints that caused them to feel uncomfortable there.

Finally, a youth group made an arrangement with the owner to rent the space for a small amount per month. Knowing some of the previous track record for renters, the group decided to handle move-in a little differently. Each person who would be working in the office went upstairs to introduce him or herself to the space. They spent a few minutes there getting the feel of the office and chatting amiably, seemingly to themselves.

Many of the group felt silly and were unaffected by the office. The two adult members, however, were quite affected. One felt the immediate stirrings of a migraine headache the minute she went into the office and backed out quickly. She did her introduction and casual chat from just outside the door. The other adult felt mildly dizzy and could not seem to make her eyes focus on specific objects. Everything had a too-sharp outline, as if up against a green screen. She did stay in the space to converse.

At last, the furniture was moved in. The office was filled slowly and with a sense of calm. For both of the adults, the odd affects passed, and business was conducted in peace.

Later the group learned that there had been a paranormal investigation conducted in the building. In this particular office, which had a label above the door calling it "Office K," strange sounds had been recorded. In one burst of sound, there was a clear voice speaking above the background static. It said, "I am Kevin." From then on, the members of the youth group always addressed Kevin by name.

The paranormal group explained that, by context of some other things that happened and were observed, Kevin may have been from the 1860s. Now that he had a name, and we had been given some vague clues as to his era, it was fun to assign attributes to Kevin. Most of the youth imagined him as a dapper gentleman who was mostly serious and polite.

Kevin must not have been the entity that inhabited the salon space. Only once was any money left in Office K, and it was only a penny. But Kevin has his own talents, and they have far-reaching effects. Kevin was adept at fiddling with the heating system. The office had a separate small furnace in a closet at the corner of the space. It was temperamental at best and often downright ornery. The repair service came several times, only to find nothing wrong and the furnace in perfect working order. After several visits, one of the adults went into the room and chided Kevin for making his guests uncomfortable. All heating problems ended.

To preface the next story, it must be pointed out that Office K sits a floor above Main Street. Main Street is also a state highway, and it is busy. There are over eight thousand cars that traverse Main Street on any given day, and not only cars but also large trucks and even larger farm equipment travel the road. It is an active street, sending lots of bumps and vibrations into the curbside businesses.

By the time of this story, the office had changed hands again, and it was occupied by a nonprofit group. The manager of the nonprofit came in to open up on a Monday morning. She sat down to begin her work for the day and stopped in surprise. There, on the corner of her desk, was a stick pen standing upright on its flat cap. It hadn't been there when she left the Friday prior, and certainly it couldn't have stood there long with heavy traffic rolling by. She was at a loss to explain.

Kevin may not have an interest in money, but he apparently has a fascination with keys and locks. For a time, I worked in Office K. I was one of the adults involved with the youth group. One evening, closing up for the day, I went down the stairs to the street door. I wondered if I should lock the door or if there were still others in the building. I decided to let it stay unlocked. The moment the decision was made, I was nearly overwhelmed by the smell of pipe smoke. There were no smokers anywhere on the street. What I smelled was the smoke of a very close pipe with a sharp, clean odor. It made me stop and then wonder where it came from. I stood for a few seconds contemplating my next move. Finally, I wondered if Kevin wanted me to lock the door. I stepped forward, slid my key into the lock and all trace of smoke evaporated. Apparently that was the right move. Kevin, the security-conscious ghost.

I had a single, silver key to Office K. It was tied with a long red ribbon for hanging up and for easy identification. The actions of that key, for a while, were very puzzling. One afternoon I walked down the sidewalk after exiting and locking the building, which required key in hand. I looked to the left and saw something glinting in the crosswalk. Feeling that it was something familiar, I went into the cross walk, stooped down and picked up my key—the one I'd just used to lock the door.

Another time I found that same key, which I thought was hung up on its assigned peg, lying at the edge of the street a half-block away from where it belonged. Again, even from a distance it was recognizable by the silver sparkle and the red ribbon. However, I cannot tell you what made me look up a half-block to see my key.

The owner of the nonprofit had an incident with one of her important keys, though not the one to Office K. She received a call from the police that a key to city hall had been found in front of that building. The key was stamped with the unique number that indicated it had been assigned to her. Please, she was asked, check to see if your key is missing. She checked, and her key was still with her. She held her key in hand and read off the numbers to the policeman. They were the same numbers that were stamped on the key found in the street. There were, said the officer, no duplicates made.

Finally is the tale of my key that I still find unbelievable. I was at a trade show in Portland and had no need of my Office K key, so it was left behind in its proper place. The other adult from the youth group was with me. When we reached the convention center, I searched for a parking place, had to go several times around and finally found a just-opened spot right by the elevator door. Lucky! We climbed out of my van and began to gather what we needed for our day at the trade show. As I shut the back hatch, I looked down and spotted something shiny under the edge of my back tire.

"I don't believe this!" I exclaimed.

"What?" said my companion.

"My key. It's here. In Portland. Under my tire."

We were both dumbfounded. But there it was. I edged the car off the key, pocketed it and went into the trade show. I have no idea how it got to Portland. But that was the last time it traveled in an unexpected way. Perhaps all its wanderlust was spent? Or maybe Kevin felt he'd made his point.

Many of the businesses in the Little Mall on Main experience the common oddities, such as the sound of opening doors, unexplained phone interference and the like. But in this building, the common is overshadowed by the unexpected in almost every corner of the edifice.

More than once people picked up their phones to make a call and heard voices already speaking on the line. A sort of spectral party line? A few clicks of the receiver helped restore the dial tone so calls could be made.

In the very busy upper story, voices are often heard when there are no people around to speak. One joyful surprise is the occasional spontaneous laughter that erupts unexpectedly in empty hallways. Footsteps are commonplace. The sense of a presence unseen is a regular phenomenon.

But I cannot leave out the street level of this building. Stories flow from ground level as well. One evening I was witness to one of the things that happened often in or near the central entryway. I was sitting with friends in a shop on the north side of the building. Suddenly, there was a bright and self-contained flash of light. It seemed to burst from the air mid-shop. The flash was on my retina as an image much longer than it was visible. The shop owner was not disturbed, saying only that it was nice when somebody beside herself saw some of these things.

She went on to tell us about other happenings. Her shop featured yarns, crafting supplies and patterns. Most mornings her first job of the day was to reshelve the things that were on the floor. Often patterns or yarns were laid out

226 South Main Street, 1915. *Courtesy Heritage Museum.*

in clever patterns, as if someone had been playing with them, admiring the colors and combinations. Sometimes things were thrown more haphazardly into the room, with much more force that a rumbling passing truck would exert. Were those days when there was some resident moodiness?

Finally, there is the story of the two offices in the back of the first floor. At the time, the back office held a printing and copying business. The forward office held a computer networking and accessories business.

In the computer business, one of the owners had been concerned with the remodeling activity going on in the back office. They had lots of accessories hung up on a shared wall, and every time the hammering and pounding began, his small groups of accessories threatened to fly off the wall from the force of the blows. One day the noise and vibration was worse than ever, and things did begin to fall from their hooks on the wall.

The computer guy went to go visit the printing shop. "So," he said. "What are you building today?"

"What do you mean?" asked the printer.

"All the banging is starting to knock things off my walls. Can you hold it down?"

"Banging?" The printer was puzzled. "There's no banging in here. We are done with construction and have been for a couple of weeks."

Here is a look down Main Street, toward the south. Messner Clothing, Dry Goods and Groceries takes up what are today the River Gallery and Ash Creek Clinic/Maxine's. Across the street is the Cooper building. Beyond that is the Little Mall on Main, before the second story was added. The Opera House stands tall in the distance. *Courtesy Heritage Museum.*

The computer guy knew that had to be true. There were no tools in evidence, no tell-tale remnants of construction. What kind of construction was going on? Through an adjoining wall, he had heard it and seen the results of the vibrations. But the printer had neither seen nor heard a thing.

The flashes of light, voices and laughter also occur in the courtyard entryway to this building. Some who have had businesses on either side of the entry would say it is the most active place in the entire site. I doubt, however, that other residents would be likely to agree.

CHAPTER 28

250 SOUTH MAIN STREET AND THE INDEPENDENCE OPERA HOUSE

Today, at 250 South Main you will find the Independence Hop & Barrel House, a cozy pub oozing with historic ambiance. Without doubt there will soon be stories to tell of the otherworldly nature, but the owners are fully concentrating on business. You can go in and have a private party in the vault, for this building, too, was once a bank. The door to the vault has been removed.

Before it was a pub, this was for many years 250 South Main Antiques and Fine Art, as depicted in the photograph on the opposite page. You could find treasures large and small in the store. One of the most unique stories coming from here concerns a set of stained-glass windows that were once a fixture here. The beautiful windows had been sold years back and were presumably lost. The storeowners would have liked to have them back in place but thought it would never happen.

Then they went to an antique show in Seattle. To their surprise, the windows—stained glass, beautiful and clearly from their building—were for sale. We don't know what they paid, but we do know the windows are back in their place and looking gorgeous.

Sometime in its history, 250 South Main was a bank or was intended to hold something of great value. There is a vault inside the building that comfortably holds ten people, plus a table and chairs. The Hop & Barrel House has taken off the door and opened this space for private parties. I'm not particularly claustrophobic, but I can't go into that area. If I get too near, I feel as if I'm being pulled in. When I look into the space, the walls look like

Now Independence Hop & Barrel House, there used to be an antiques store at 250 South Main Street. *Courtesy the author.*

they're moving, and the room is getting smaller. I can sit comfortably outside of the room, but I have never been in it and never will.

THE INDEPENDENCE OPERA HOUSE

The Opera House has hidden beauty. I have known it to be a basket shop and a furniture and appliance store. I had no idea that a lovely performance area was tucked in upstairs. It has beautiful tongue-and-groove floors, a

Independence Opera House, South Main Street. *Courtesy Ted Baker.*

cloakroom and a small kitchen. Tall, rounded windows overlook the streets. In its day, this was the formal dance hall in Independence. It was the site of coming-out parties, formal dances, USO evenings and theater performances. According to an article by Gail Oberst in the August 19, 2008 edition of the *Itemizer-Observer* newspaper:

> *The upstairs floor was known originally as "Independence Opera House" and then as "Sloper's Hall" from the 1920s to the 1960s. In that time, it hosted a variety of events and gatherings, including plays, performances and dances. Since the 1960s, it has been used for storage.*
>
> *The downstairs floor has housed retail shops. It was divided into two stores until 1968. The stores once located in the building include: J.L. Stockton, Williams' Drug, Patterson's Drug, Metropolitan Dry*

Goods, Sloper Hardware, Amsberry Variety, V's Variety, Scranton's Variety, a basket shop, Independence Hardware, Western Auto, and Independence Appliance.

The building has already undergone two complete storefront replacements. The first was completed prior to 1930. The second was completed in 1968.

According to one report in Oregon Curiosities, Quirky Characters, Roadside Oddities & Other Offbeat Stuff, *the building was the site of an electrical display aimed at allaying the fears of townsfolk still reticent about the safety of electricity. In 1891, 16-year-old Lulu Nye of Newport was crowned Miss Electricity and draped in a string of light bulbs at her waist, as a crown and on her scepter. The article said Miss Electricity was introduced at a carnival being held in the newly wired opera house. "Miss Miller…stepped forward and suddenly was enveloped in a flood of light… The audience was so enthusiastic that a recall was necessary."*

Families who have lived in Independence for many years remember the Opera House events. Those who served in earlier wars remember the USO dances that were so joyous.

One World War II vet told us that the USO dances at the Opera House were real events. Tables and chairs were set up around the room. Someone in the cloakroom took your outer garments and gave you a small metal number to hold. There was food and drink and live music. These were events!

In contrast, town dances and USO gatherings were also held at Green Villa Barn. Today, Green Villa Barn has been beautifully restored and is a wonderful venue for large gatherings, formal and informal. But back in earlier times, it was a rougher, more rustic destination. There was a band shell that helped a band fill the barn with music. Instead of tables and chairs, people sat on bales of hops. We can imagine the floor covered with hay, and the place being pretty hot in the summer and equally cold when the temperature dropped. It was the country place to gather.

The Opera House is in the process of full and very careful restoration. The owner is meticulous in finding the right colors to match the building's original look. The street-level part of the structure has been divided in two spaces. Already one of the spaces, fully restored, holds a great restaurant. The other is waiting for just the right tenant before it is finished. Upstairs, the Opera House also waits for its new finish. When you look at the building from the street, there is a feeling of waiting. We think the building is waiting to be glorious and important once again.

CHAPTER 29
TAYLOR'S DRUG

The Taylor's building was constructed in 1884 by financiers H. Hirschberg and Rosendorf. Hirschberg was a prominent businessperson and built the Independence National Bank in 1889. An agricultural merchandising store was located in the building to begin with. By 1888, a hardware store had replaced the agricultural store, and a small addition was built onto the rear of this building.

Max Goldmen owned a grocery store located in the building in 1913. Sylvester Drug occupied the building in the 1930s and was purchased by the Taylors in 1944. The drugstore has been an important gathering place for the citizens of Independence and still retains a soda and lunch counter. The store also had an extensive collection of authentic Coca-Cola trays, believed to be one of the larger collections in the country. Taylor's closed in 2006 after over sixty years in business.

Taylor's Drug is closed now, but it was a cornerstone in downtown Independence for fifty years. Mr. Taylor, a good businessman, opened the store in the late 1940s. He listened to what people needed and wanted and then fulfilled those needs and wants with stock in his store.

Taylor's had an authentic soda fountain and was mixing milkshakes the old-fashioned way right up to its last day in business. It had strings for your violin, valve oil for your trumpet and those hateful gym uniforms. Taylor's carried Boy Scout gear, greeting cards, gag gifts and lovely presents for your mother. A full lunch was served at its counter, and if you were a regular, your sandwich was on the grill before you had to ask. Mrs. Taylor made sure

Taylor's Drug building, 1915. For many years, Taylor's was a traditional soda fountain. *Courtesy Heritage Museum.*

the windows were always dressed for the season and featured the newest wares. Taylor's was on top of all the crazes from hula-hoops to pet rocks, reproduction antique toys to Beanie Babies. There was a pharmacy in the back. In short, Taylor's was the place to go to get what you needed. And if the Taylors didn't have it, they would get it.

There was a time when a couple young guys tried to take advantage of Taylor's varied stock. They knew about the drugs behind the pharmacy counter in the back. They also knew something else: Taylor's had a roof access that wasn't locked.

The guys hatched a plan to get into Taylor's before sunrise, when the streets were still quiet. They would find the attic entry, open it, go into the pharmacy and collect something they could sell for good cash money. Then they would exit the way they had come in, and nobody would suspect a thing until the drugs were found to be missing. By then they'd blend into the crowd and would get away scot-free.

In those days, the police station was in a building right behind Taylor's. Police got calls about crimes, and citizens also brought in reports and information. But another great way to know what was going on in town was to open the door and step out. They were a few feet away from the main downtown intersection, and a lot could be seen and heard from there.

Back to our budding criminals. One night they did find their way up on the roof and down into Taylor's by way of the unlocked access. They dropped into the attic and began to look for the opening into the store. Apparently, however, they had no experience walking in attics. Most everybody knows that when you're in an attic you walk on the stringers. What's between the stringers is often not strong enough to hold any weight. In their ignorance, the guys began walking toward the back of the store. It didn't take long before each of them broke through and landed, high-centered, on a stringer.

Oh, the shouting! It was loud enough to be heard from the police station. Police, in those days, often had copies of every business's key, in case there was an incident that required immediate entry. Judging from the noise, there was quite an incident going on inside Taylor's. By now, morning was getting closer, and soon the sun would be creeping up over the trees. The officer on duty grabbed the key to Taylor's and went to take a look.

It didn't take him long to surmise what had happened. There were two pairs of legs hanging through the ceiling, feet were pointing toward the back of the store, aiming at the pharmacy. Clearly, entry had not been through the front door. After a quick assessment, the policeman called out, "See you in the morning, boys," and promptly left.

In an unwitting parallel to this story, the Taylors for years had a "half a Santa" that decorated their store at Christmas. It was just Santa's lower half, suspended from the ceiling to look like he'd made it halfway through the chimney.

CHAPTER 30
ONE MORE FOR THE (RAIL)ROAD

Here our Ghost Walk ends. We've visited a lot of places and heard a lot of stories. I am proud of our stories. It does not matter if they have an edge of creativity or if they are always politically correct. Stories are traded, shared and likely embellished with the telling. Stories become things to be owned and valued by individuals and by communities. Communities embrace their stories because they say something about the community itself. They speak to values, to hearts and to humor. They are something to be cherished and polished. Whether individual or community, county or nation, stories give us identity. How we capture and claim the stories, how we hold them close and when we care enough about someone to share our stories—on this foundation is our personality, even our integrity, built. What are your stories? Have you shared a story today? It's good for the soul.

One more story, one that speaks about our community of Independence.

The railroad track runs right down the center of Second Street in Independence. Some of the corners on this street are so old that they still have a metal edging, installed to keep the concrete from tearing up wagon wheels and vice versa.

The railroad tracks on Second Street have been an abominable mess. For as far back as I am aware, the city has been asking the railroad to fix the tracks on Second Street. A recent survey was sent to citizens asking what they'd like to see happen in their city for the betterment of the community. One of the top three answers: "Fix the tracks on Second Street."

The city recorder, by law, must open records to the public once a year. A few years ago, the city recorder was preparing for this "open house" and decided to make the event more interesting. She went looking through old city correspondence to find fun things. She stumbled on one handwritten letter addressed from the mayor and council to the railroad. It said, in effect, "Please fix the tracks on Second Street." The letter was dated 1894.

It seems Independence's quest for better tracks has been going on for a while.

Meanwhile, there was another story was running parallel. The railroad—or its employees, at least—were trying to fix the tracks on Second Street. The only problem was that when someone set up the work order to fix the tracks, his employment was terminated soon after.

In the 1990s, everything looked to be ready, but before work could start, the employee who gave the go-ahead was fired, and the project scrapped.

In the early part of this century, another railroad executive tackled the problem. A work plan was made, the order given and the executive was terminated. The project died again.

We all began to wonder how long this had been going on. After all, we'd been asking for better tracks since 1894. Had there been a whole string of railroad employees let go because of our request?

Even with that question, the tracks got worse by the day, and fixing them was becoming more and more of a necessity. At last, one more brave railroad executive jumped into the fray. But he was smart. He made a deal with the city manager that went like this:

"I'll get your railroad fixed. But I'm going to use some unusual methods to make it happen. To make it work, you have to do something for me. If somebody asks how you managed to get the tracks fixed, you must reply, 'We just got up one morning and the tracks were fixed. We don't know how it happened!' Agreed?"

The city manager agreed, and the work was, at last, done. To our knowledge, the railroad exec still has his job.

So now, on Ghost Walk night, when groups are shown the metal strips on the curbs and told their purpose, we also tell the tale of the tracks. Our guests get brought into the conspiracy, too. They must promise that if somewhere, sometime, they are asked, "How did Independence get the railroad tracks fixed?" they must answer, "We don't know. One morning they were just fixed. It's a mystery."

CHAPTER 31

COMMUNITY SPIRIT

S tories define us. For a city, it is no different. Stories that are shared remind citizens that each community has heart, a sense of humor and a pride in its heritage. They outline for resident and visitor alike what the city is all about. Stories have so much texture that they can contain dozens— even hundreds—of messages.

Let me share with you a community story and tell you what it means to me.

A soldier came to town during the middle days of World War II. He was stationed at Camp Adair, which is between Independence and Corvallis, Oregon. Camp Adair was a training ground for soldiers who would later be shipped overseas. The army had designed a part of Camp Adair to mirror a German town. The soldiers would carry out exercises in the mock town, preparing them through sight and sound for the real thing.

The particular soldier's name was John. He had been a teacher in his home state of Iowa, but he had signed up to serve his country in the war effort. John lived at Camp Adair during his training, but on weekends and leave times, he went into Independence. He went to the USO events, walked and visited all around town and had a grand time.

One evening he met a young lady named Marjorie at a USO dance. Maybe it wasn't at first sight, but it was love pretty quickly. John shipped out, did his duty and came back to Independence and to Marjorie. They got married.

John started an insurance business. He sold insurance locally and took care of his clients carefully. Some of the riskier things that John insured were hop kilns. These wooden structures were built to dry the harvested hops. In order to bring the process along, fires were built underneath the floors where the hops dried. Hop kilns were a high risk because of the fire/wood combination. But John took his chances and, in fact, watched a few of them burn. The occasional loss did not deter him, because he knew that he was providing a service needed by the community.

John got involved in the community. He joined the Masonic lodge in Independence and was a worthy member for the rest of his life. He joined the American Legion and served as commander several times. He even provided a place for meetings in a piece of property he acquired downtown.

Another thing that happened right away was involvement with youth. He "had his arm twisted," as he recalled with a smile, and was appointed a Boy Scout leader. He did this job as he would any other job—to the best of his ability, giving what he felt his troop needed.

John also got involved in politics. I don't suppose it was deliberate but probably started with a suggestion, an idea and finally an agreement. John's political career peaked when he served as mayor of Independence for several years.

I met John when he was in his early eighties. He was still an active participant in community. He had his rounds that he went on every day, visiting various shops and neighbors just to check in to see how life was going.

Though he was not a Boy Scout leader anymore, he had mentored hundreds of scouts over the years. Many were still in town, now adults who ran businesses and raised families. They were in contact with John, kidding him about how "old" he must be, since he was their scout leader, and they were themselves seniors.

John was still active in politics. Though he held no office, he was always on the lookout for folks who would make good council and commission members. He didn't coerce, but he suggested, often, and reminded his candidate how grateful the community would be to have their help in some public position.

John may have read papers and listened to news. But he did something even more effective: he engaged his community daily. He knew lots of folks, could tell lots of stories and loved his town.

Twelve years ago, I was approached about being on city council. The suggestion came from Mayor McArdle, but John wasted no time in getting involved. He told me (didn't ask—told me) that he would be my campaign manager. He would take care of getting the petition, getting all the signatures and turning in my papers at the right time and place to get my name on the ballot.

Mayor John Pfaff. *Courtesy City of Independence, photo collection of mayors.*

My misstep was not paying enough attention to his statement. John was an old guy by then, and driving was getting more difficult. I didn't want him driving to our county seat, ten miles away, navigating the courthouse to collect a petition and then driving back. I felt I should take care of at least that much and maybe get a couple of signatures myself.

When I had done those things, then I turned the petition over to John with three signatures already in place. When I gave these things to him, John was crushed. He had—to his way of thinking—promised that he would do all that. He felt like he'd let me down.

When I came up for reelection, I knew better than to do anything that my campaign manager would prefer to get done himself. He was four years older but allowed no change to his original plan. He and his battered truck drove to the county seat and did everything for me. He did let me sign my own petition.

One of the shining moments in John's later life was having a park named for him. The city had set aside park space not yet developed. The Parks and Rec commission carefully decided about park amenities, gathering volunteer helpers and ordering equipment. It spent very little time deciding the name for the park. It wasn't common practice to name a park after a living individual, but folks in Independence do what they think is best. The park was finished and christened John Pfaff Park. John was there with his children and grandchildren to celebrate the day. Also there were many, many former Boy Scouts who had been in John's care.

This last time I ran for reelection, I had no campaign manager because John had passed away the year before at age ninety-three. I felt like I was

Independence, looking down Main and C Streets. *Courtesy Heritage Museum.*

Panoramic view of Independence, 1911, at Main and C Streets. Paved roads were five years in the future. *Courtesy Heritage Museum.*

betraying a trust when I went to get my own paperwork and collected my own signatures.

What meaning does this story hold for me? It tells me that you can act independently and achieve great results if you have the best interests of your community at heart. It tells me that home is where you decide it will be, but that you have to tend and nurture the concept. It tells me, too, that connections with community have to be regularly stirred. Finally, the story reminds me that there is love in every corner of the place you have made for yourself, as long as you are willing to reach out and make contact.

John Pfaff is one of my private shining stars and a role model that I recall often and with fondness. He is the center of one of the best stories to come out of my community.

APPENDIX I

OPERATING A GHOST WALK

The Ghost Walk has achieved a measure of local fame. The day before I put these particular words to paper, a friend was at the coast at a city fifty-five miles away from Independence. He was in a restaurant, and someone heard him mention Independence. The listener asked, "Do you still do that great Ghost Walk in Independence?" Word travels.

Three years ago, I received a call from a woman in Ohio. She had been visiting Independence in late September and had taken the Ghost Walk with her relatives. It turns out she had a Sunday radio show in Ohio and wanted to include Ghost Walk stories on her broadcast. She requested a copy of a souvenir booklet, which was sent to her. I have not heard from her since, but somewhere out in rural Ohio, folks know about our Ghost Walk.

Since the first year, we have people who have been on every single Ghost Walk. Attracting guests does not seem to be difficult, but recruiting volunteer hosts often is. As attendance has grown, organizing the Ghost Walk has evolved into a rather complicated endeavor. Today we need more than forty people every year to give their time to lead a Ghost Walk and provide support services. Leaders are trained and retrained yearly so they have all the latest information. Group leaders are called Ghost Hosts. In plans for expansion currently being considered, we hope to add some actors to pantomime some of stories told by Hosts. There is full reliance on volunteers. For its first eleven years, at least, the Ghost Walk has been a free event, though donations are gladly accepted.

Planning begins months in advance of the actual Ghost Walk. Site and host recruitment has already happened. There are some very dedicated volunteers who help with the Ghost Walk, primarily site hosts and tour hosts.

Site recruitment is an easy task now, as business owners/managers ask to be a part of the Ghost Walk. But in the early days, it took a little more persuasion. After all, an official site on the Ghost Walk has some responsibility to the success of the event. A designated speaker must be on site to share the stories of their location. He or she may talk to fifteen or more groups in an evening. There will be repetition, but reading from a script is not encouraged. Stories are better told than read. Each group of walkers brings unique questions and comments, and these are often rich with local lore. The location is also "open" for the Ghost Walk, meaning some business may be done as well. It calls for a site host to be fast on his or her feet. Guests love talking to the business owner, as well as having stories from the hosts. It is not uncommon for a speaker at a site to bring up something new that has happened recently. These are the hardest bits to manage. We don't want these nuggets to be forgotten.

In order to keep everyone up to date on what is happening, we have a "story swap" evening every couple of years. Site hosts are invited to tell stories, spectral or anecdotal, that might be interesting to the fabric of the Ghost Walk.

The great recruiting movement for Ghost Hosts never ends. If one thousand people come to the Ghost Walk (a regular occurrence!), and we want to keep our tour groups to thirty, the truly maximum size for walk-and-talk tours, then we need at least thirty-three hosts. As the creator of all of this, I have pledged to take the last group to go, trying to collect the latecomers. More than once I have started with a group of one hundred. But I don't worry about that anymore. Something always seems to happen to help out. One year, a trained host, not planning to participate that year, materialized at an opportune time and took a part of my group.

APPENDIX II

BRINGING STORIES AND PEOPLE TOGETHER

Who can be a Ghost Host?

Ghost Hosts come from all cultures. It is a special addition to have a host who is bilingual. But in the absence of that, Ghost Hosts are trained to ask a language-capable guest to assist with translation when needed. There is never any group sorting or matching. Guests are put into groups as they arrive. Hosts are always flexible. If a guest or group of guests wants to change hosts, to jump into a group already en route or to drop out early because they are tired, it's all OK.

One aspect of Ghost Host training is encouragement in getting group participation. Makeup of a tour group is usually varied. As a Host, I ask for help in many ways. Middle-school age kids are great "herders." They seem to have an innate talent for keeping groups moving and together. I bless those who show up in my groups and put them to work. Elders are a source of history in the very midst of the group. They are usually great at sharing, having left shyness behind them long ago. Out of town guests bring stories of other places to a group, helping to energize the longer stretches of walking.

I am most careful to listen to the group at large, because the local folks enjoy the Ghost Walk, too. And they share local stories! "I remember when..." "Once when I was little..." "My dad told me one time..."—these are all cues that a good story could be coming, one good for group sharing and often specific enough that it can be included in a future Ghost Walk.

Remember, the rule is to be able to say, "I heard that..."

Downtown Independence, circa 1911. *Courtesy Heritage Museum.*

Training Ghost Hosts is a lengthy process. Training sessions are scheduled, and people show up as they are able. Hosts always want to be retrained for the current year because new information is constantly being added to the text of the tour. Though it started with just three stops, there are now thirty points of interest along the Ghost Walk route. To "train" a host, we go over the entire Ghost Walk route, without entering any buildings or speaking to site hosts. This process, done at a very fast-paced walk, takes between seventy-five and ninety minutes. When Hosts gather their groups on Ghost Walk night, they will be visiting only half of the sites on the tour. Sites are divided into two groupings, and a Host will take his group to either the first or second set of sites. If sites keep being added to the Ghost Walk, we will soon have to create three distinct routes. To visit only half of the sites, the average group needs two hours. Groups, by their very nature, must go at the pace of the slowest member.

When the big night arrives, hosts check in and connect with guests who will be in their groups. Hosts are issued bullhorns if they need some amplification for their guests. They already have received their official host scripts, which were delivered when they were trained.

There are all types of community stories shared on Ghost Walk night. Some are modern; some are older. Some are anecdotal, some historic and many are spectral. These stories bind my community together with a common memory and a shared sense of uniqueness. It is always a pleasure for me to share these stories or to swap them like trading cards.

ABOUT THE AUTHOR

Marilyn Morton has lived in Independence since 1990. She was raised in Pendleton, another town full of stories. Marilyn and her husband, Victor, came to Independence from Salem. They wanted to find a place to become more civically involved, and it worked. Marilyn sits on the Independence City Council and is a member of many other boards and committees, including the Independence Hop and Heritage Festival Commission. Victor runs a small business downtown and is a longtime member of the Masonic lodge. They have three diverse and delightful children, several grandchildren and many cats.

Visit us at
www.historypress.net

···

This title is also available as an e-book